Learn Python

Programming

A complete guide to learning Python basics and it's practical applications in recent development technologies

By

Anthony Wallit

Contents

Introduction 8

Chapter 1: Introduction to Python 10
   1.1: About Python 10
   1.2: History of Python 12
   1.3: Drawbacks of Python 14
   1.4: Installation 17
   1.5: Guidelines for Good Programming 21

Chapter 2: Python Data Types 27
   2.1: Mutable Data Type 29
   2.2: List in Python 30
   2.3: Python Sets 31
   2.4: Dictionary In Python 33
   2.5: Immutable Data Types 34
   2.6: Numeric Data Types 36
   2.7: Tuple 37

Chapter 3: Loops and Conditional Statements 42
   3.1: Conditional Programming 42
   3.2: Loops 53

Chapter 4: Python Functions 58
   4.1: Using Functions and their Return Values 60
   4.2: Recursive Function 63

Chapter 5: Object-Oriented Programming In Python 66

5.1: Python Class 67
5.2: Classes And Instances 69
5.3: Inherit From Other Classes in Python 70
5.4: Variables in Python 70
5.5: Polymorphism in Python 74
5.6: Python's Operator Overloading 76

Chapter 6: List and Built-in Functions 78
6.1: Lists 78
6.2: Tuples 87
6.3: Built-in Functions 90

Chapter 7: File Handling 94
7.1: Editing Files 95
7.2: Directory Contents 102

Chapter 8: Exception Handling In Python 104
8.1: Try And Except 106
8.2: Exception Handling For A Specific Exception 107
8.3: Try And Else Clause In Exception Handling 107
8.4: Keyword In Exception Handling 108
8.5: Raising Exception 108
8.6: Advantages of Exception Handling 109

Chapter 9: Data Science and Python 111
9.1: Jupyter Notebook 114
9.2: Data Dealing 122
9.3: DataFrames 125

Chapter 10: Python and Game Development 131
    10.1: Game Development Process 133
    10.2: Game Coding 135
    10.3: Python Frameworks 139
    10.4: Pygame Python 142
    10.5: Pygame vs. Arcade Coding 143

Chapter 11: GUI in Python 145
    11.1: Building Your First GUI With Tkinter 146
    11.2: Making Your Applications Interactive 155
    11.3: Building a Temperature Converter 157

Chapter 12: Python and Web Development 161
    12.1: Frameworks 164
    12.2: Django basics 167
    12.3: Future of web development 169

Conclusion 173

Introduction

Python is a powerful, object-oriented, rising software program with dynamic semantics that may be executed on a computer's desktop. High-level data structures and the dynamic type and binding make it an extremely attractive choice for Faster Development and a scripting or bridge language for connecting existing components.

As a result of Python's support for modules and packages, program modularity & code reuse are encouraged. Guus van Rossum worked just at National Research Center for Computer science Netherlands during the late 1980s and early nineties when he invented the Python programming language. Python is derived from various programming languages, including ABC, Unit, C, C++, Algol-68, Smalltalk, the Unix shell, and other scripting languages.

Python is a programming language written in Python. Intellectual property rights protect Python. Python code has become available as an Open Public License, just like Perl source code (GPL). Even though Guido van Rossum continues to play an important role in the development of Python, the language is now kept by a team of developers at the institute. Python is extensively used for online and software development, task automation, data processing, and visualization.

Python has been accepted by many non-programmers, such as economists and scientists, since it is amazingly simple to learn and can be used for various common tasks, such as arranging financial records. Python isn't just for coders and data scientists; it's also for everyone. Learning Python can open up new opportunities for those who work in less data-intensive fields, such as journalists, small businesspeople, and social media marketers.

Chapter 1: Introduction to Python

1.1: About Python

Python is a high, object-oriented, increased software program with dynamic semantics that may be executed on a computer's desktop. High-level data structures and the dynamic type and binding make it a particularly appealing choice as Rapid Application Development and a programming or glue language for connecting existing components. As a result of Python's support for modules and packages, program modularity or code reuse are encouraged.

Python is often hailed as the programming language of choice by programmers due to its enhanced productivity. Given the lack of a compilation phase, the modification cycle is fast and efficient. Debugging Python applications is straightforward since a bug or erroneous input will never result in a segmentation fault. An exception is thrown instead of a warning when the interpreter discovers a mistake. When a program fails to catch an exception, the interpreter outputs a stack trace of what happened. A source-level debugging provides the examination of locally and globally variables, the evaluation of random expressions, the setting of breakpoints, the walking through the code one line at a time, and many other features that are not available in a runtime debugger. The debugger is developed entirely in Python, demonstrating the reflective capabilities of the language. The basic strategy of adding a few print lines in the source code, on either hand, is frequently the quickest way to identify a program: the rapid modification cycle makes this approach particularly successful.

Python is a potent, general-purpose coding language that may be used for various tasks. Its enterprise idea emphasizes computer code readability, which is achieved by using substantial indentation.

Python is a dynamically typed and garbage-collected programming language. In respect of its vast standard library, it is sometimes referred to as a "battery packs included" language. Python is commonly ranked as one of the most widely used programming languages today.

1.2: History of Python

Python was established as a substitute for the ABC software design language in the late 1980s, and its execution began in late 1989 with Guido van Rossum of CWI within the Netherlands as an exception-handling programming language capable of connecting with the Amoeba computer system. Benevolent Dictator for Living is the title given to Van Rossum by the Python community to reflect his ongoing central role in determining the direction of Python. Van Rossum is the principal author of Python. His ongoing central role in deciding the orientation of Python is mirrored in the label given to him by this same Python community BDFL. (On the other hand, van Rossum resigned from his position as head in 2018.) Python was given its name in honor of the BBC television program

Monty Python's Fly Circus.

Many key new features were introduced with Python 2.0, which was published on October 16, 2000. These included a cycle-detecting debugger for memory support and management for Unicode characters. Nonetheless, the most significant change included the design process, which was transformed into a more open and community-supported approach.

On December 3, 2008, Python 3.0, a significant, backward-incompatible update, was made available to the public following a lengthy testing period. It has also been international and regional to Python 2.6 and 2.7, which are still backward compatible, but the Python development team is no longer maintained.

Van Rossum made the code available to the outsourced mailing list in February 1991. At this point in the development process, there were already classes with inheritance and exception handling in place and functions and the fundamental data types of lists, dict, str, and so on. Another feature included in this first edition was a module system derived from Modula-3; Van Rossum characterizes the modules as "one of Python's core programming units." Although it differs from Modula-3's exception model, Python's exception model is similar in that it includes an else clause. Comp.lang.python, the principal

discussion forum of Python, was established in 1994, marking a watershed moment in developing the language's user base.

1.3: Drawbacks of Python

Python has a high degree of abstraction that is frequently used. This programming language is extensively utilized by developers across various areas, from web development to computer vision. On the other hand, Python comes with several pros and downsides.

Speed: It is a high language, which means it is slower than C/C++ or Java compared to other programming languages. In contrast to C or C++, Python is not closer to the hardware since it is a strong language. Because Python computer code is managed line by line, as we have seen, it is slower than code that has been compiled and executed properly. However, as we have seen, Python instruction is compiled with the assistance of an interpreter rather than a compiler, which forces it to be slower. For every coder, the need for speed is a critical component of any project. On either hand, it can be observed that it is also quick for various web-based applications.

Even though Python is powerful in traditional desktop

platforms, which means it is an outstanding server-side language, Python is not a good language for mobile

development, implying it is a weak language for developing apps. Python is a good language for desktop development, but it is poor for developing mobile applications. It is very seldom used in mobile application development. It is why only a small number of mobile apps, such as Carbonnelle, which has a built-in Python interpreter, are written in it.

Memory Consumption: Python is not a suitable fit for any work that requires a lot of memory. Python's memory usage is likewise high, which may be attributed to the fact that the data types are quite flexible.

Access to databases: Python is a solid programming language that causes the least amount of stress and worry. However, this language is very vulnerable, and it should only be used at one's own risk. There are several limits to Python's database access while using it. When compared to common database access technologies such as JDBC or ODBC, it is discovered that Python's data access layer is immature and basic in contrast. It is a serious roadblock when large corporations are looking for a vocabulary that can allow for the seamless interaction of complicated legacy data. The Python data access layer, on the other hand, is not used by organizations that need seamless interaction with complicated historical data. In other words, it is more often used in large corporations.

Runtime Errors: This system's most significant disadvantage is its design with several flaws. Python programmers are confronted with several challenges relating to the language's design. The dynamic typing of this language necessitates extra testing, yet it also includes faults that only manifest themselves at runtime as a result of its dynamic typing.

Difficulty Learning or Performing in Other Programming Languages: Python enthusiasts grow so acclimated to the language's capabilities and huge libraries that they have difficulty learning or functioning in other computer languages.

Python may be a source of concern. Because of its easy syntax, a programmer is more likely to be a Python person, and as a result, they may believe that code written in a more difficult language such as Java is superfluous. As a result of Python's late-binding model equations and vast libraries, the author believes that switching to a new dialect from Python becomes challenging since the user has a tough time adjusting to the language's susceptible nature and treating everything with levity.

1.4: Installation

Simple coding/programming language Python, which may be downloaded, is a good starting point. Below is a step-by-step instruction for installation:

Installation using Windows 11 (version 2.1)

Python programming is straightforward and basic, but you must first ensure that Python is professionally installed on your computer to launch any Python program or application. Let us look at where to download Python on something like a Windows 11 computer.

Stage 1

Download the latest version for Windows

Download Python 3.10.0

We'll need to download the most recent Python version from the Internet to get started. By clicking on the download link below, you will be sent to the official Python download page, where you may download Python. After that, click on the yellow download link to begin the Python download process.

The following is the download link:

https://www.python.org/downloads/

Once the transferor download is complete, browse where the file was saved and double-click the ".exe" file downloaded. If a little question displays, choose "yes" to proceed with the Python installation process.

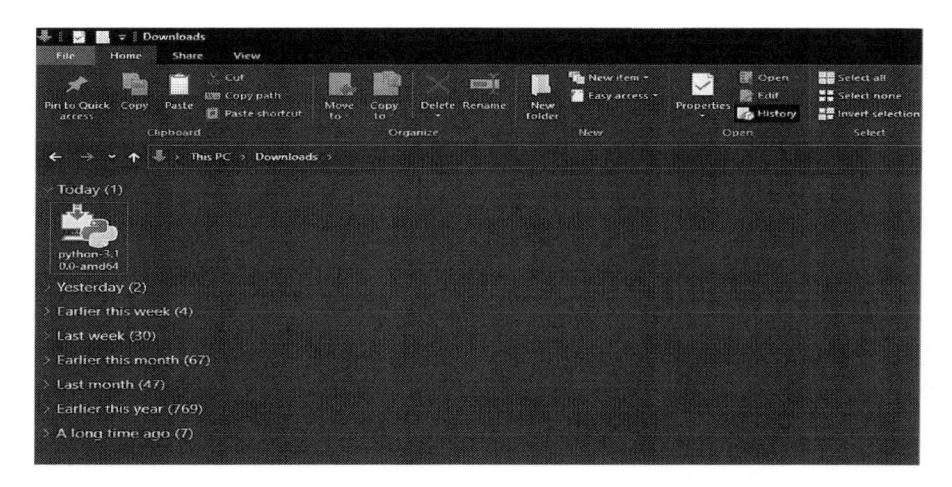

Stage 2

Following that, during the Python installation procedure, choose the choice to "Customize Installation."

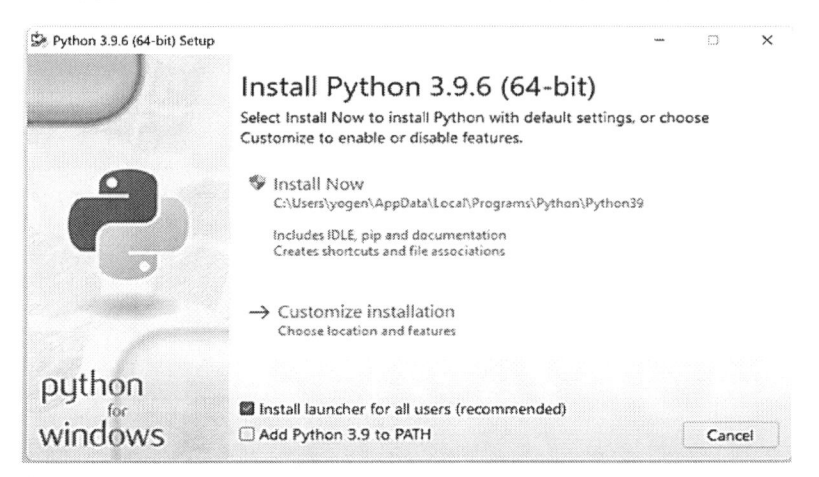

A popup window with extra features will appear; check all boxes and click the Next Button to proceed with the process.

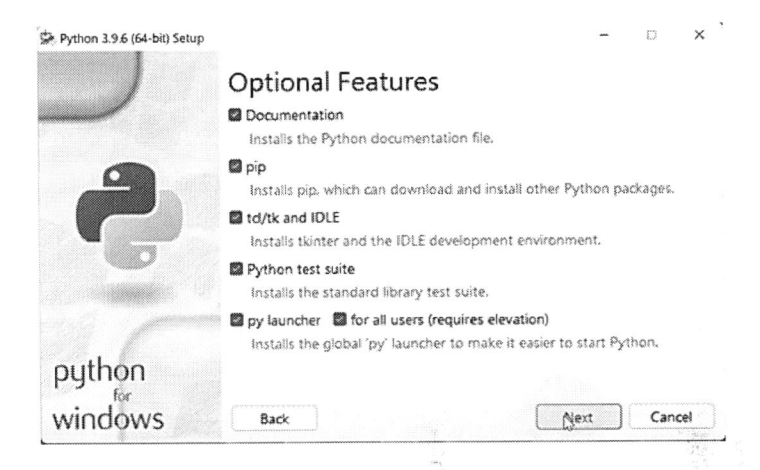

The first four checkboxes on the Advanced Settings option should be ticked as indicated.

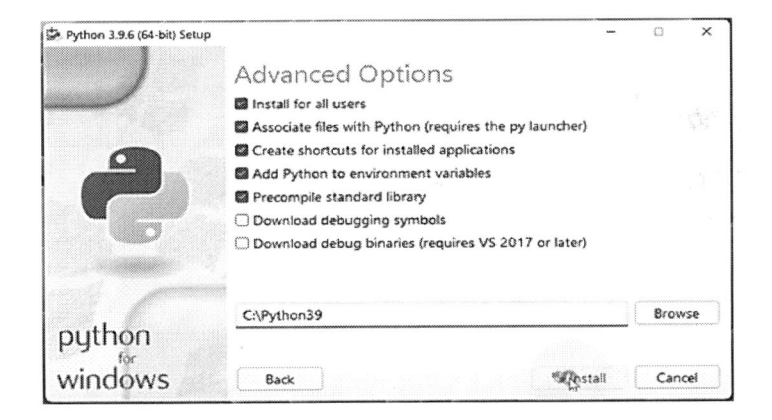

To begin your installation process, type "C: Python39" into the little text box and then click only on the register button to start the process.

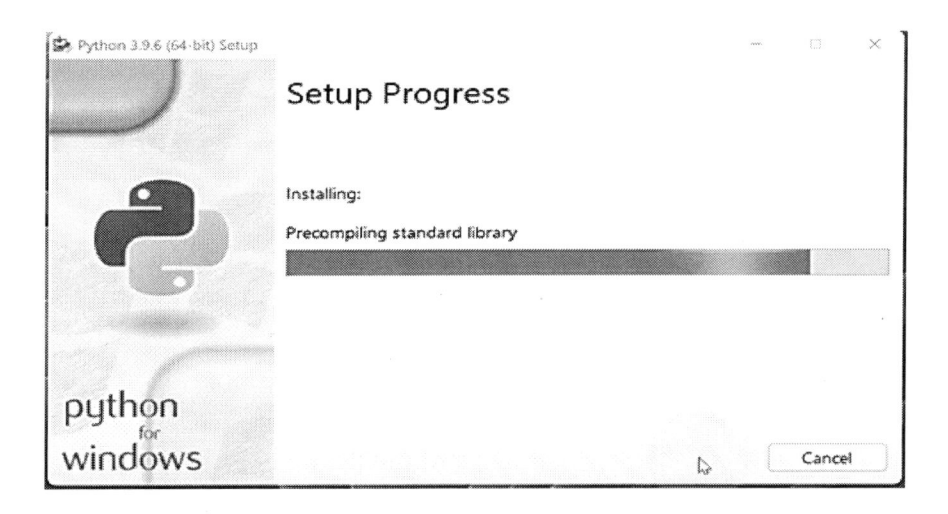

It will start the Python installation process; click on the close button to dismiss the window when it has finished successfully.

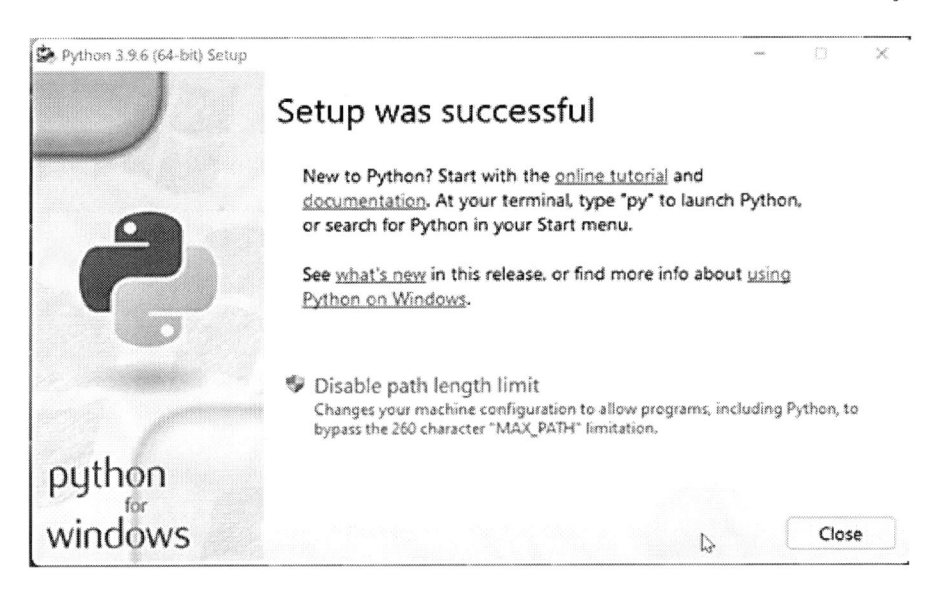

To bring up the control line, click the Windows logo, type "cmd" inside the search box, and push enter to start the control promptly.

Stage 3

Use the command prompt to type "python," then press enter; when you obtain results similar to the ones shown below, you have finally deployed Python on your Windows 11 machine and should be pleased with yourself.

1.5: Guidelines for Good Programming

The Coding phase involves coding the various modules indicated in the design specification following the module specification. After the designing phase is completed, the primary purpose of the coding stage is to develop code from the design specification created after the design step is finished and then evaluate this code.

Good software development firms use code standards to ensure that their programmers adhere to a well-defined and uniform coding style while developing software. In most cases, they build their code standards and guidelines based on what works best for their business and the sorts of software they produce. Programmers must adhere to coding standards; otherwise, the code would be rejected during the code review process.

The Purpose of Coding Standards:

- Coding standards ensure that the codes developed by various engineers have a consistent look.
- It enhances the readability and ease of maintenance of the code and reduces the overall complexity.
- It facilitates code reuse and makes it easier to identify errors.
- It encourages excellent programming principles and helps programmers work more efficiently.

The following are among the coding standards:

Global variables are used sparingly:

- These guidelines specify which kinds of data may be labeled global and which cannot.
- Headers for many modules that are standard.

The headers of distinct modules should follow a common structure and information for easier understanding or maintenance of the code. The header template must have the following items, which are often utilized in different companies:

- The module's name
- Author of the module, date of creation
- History of changes
- The module's synopsis describes what the module performs.
- The module supports several functions, each with its own set of input and output parameters.
- Module-accessible or modifiable global variables

Local variables, environment variables, constants, and functions use the following naming conventions:

The following are some of the name conventions:

- Using variables with meaningful and intelligible names

makes it easier for everyone to understand why they are being used.

- Local variables must be named in the capital case, with a tiny letter at the beginning (e.g., local Data), but global variables must be named with an uppercase (e.g., Global Data). Only capital letters should be used to construct constant names (e.g., CONSDATA).

- It's preferable to avoid using digits in placeholders.

- The function names should begin with tiny letters and be typed in a capital case.

- The function's name must clearly and succinctly convey why the function is being used.

Indentation:

Appropriate indentation is critical for improving code readability. Programmers should appropriately use white spaces to make their code understandable. The following are some examples of spacing conventions:

- After a comma, there has to be a space between two function parameters.

- Each nested block must be indented and spaced correctly.

- Each cycle in the program should have a proper indentation at the beginning or finish.
- All braces should begin on a new line, and the code after the braces should also begin on a new line.

Return values for errors and conventions for handling exceptions:

- To make debugging easier, any methods that meet an error situation should return either 0 or 1.
- On the other hand, coding guidelines provide some basic recommendations for a coding style to improve the code's understandability and readability.

The following are among the coding guidelines:

Use a code style that isn't too tough to comprehend:

The code should be simple to comprehend. Maintenance and debugging are tough and costly due to the sophisticated code.

Avoid using the same identifier for different purposes:

Each variable should have a descriptive and relevant name that explains why it is being used. It is not feasible when one identifier is used for several reasons, and the reader may get confused. Furthermore, it makes future upgrades more difficult.

Well-documented code is essential:

The code is well so that it is easy to comprehend. The code is made more understandable by adding comments to the statements.

The length of procedures should be kept to a minimum:

Long functions are quite tough to comprehend. As a result, functions should be tiny enough to do little tasks, and larger functions should be split into smaller ones to complete minor tasks.

Avoid using the GOTO statement:

The GOTO statement causes the program to become unstructured, making it harder to comprehend and debug.

Chapter 2: Python Data Types

A fundamental idea in the Python language is the concept of data types. Every value in Python has its unique data type, distinct from other data types. Information about data types is defined as classifying datasets or assigning a data value to a certain data category. It aids in understanding the types of activities to be conducted on a value. Consider our data science accreditation from top colleges if you are a newbie who wants to learn much more about the field of data science. Everything in the Python is represented as an object. Python's data types represent the various classes that exist. Variables are used to refer to the entities or instances of these classes. Let's look at the many sorts of data types available in Python. In Python, every variable contains a single instance of the object. There are two sorts of objects in Python: Immutable and mutable objects. When an object is created, it is given a unique item id that can be used to identify it. When an object is created, its type is determined at runtime, and it cannot be modified after that. If it is a changeable object, on the other hand, its state can be altered.

```
                        Python DataTypes
      ┌──────┬──────────┬──────┬──────┬──────────────┐
   Numeric  Dictionary Boolean Set   Sequence Type
   ┌──┼──┐                            ┌────┬────┐
Integer Float Complex No.         Strings List Tuple
```

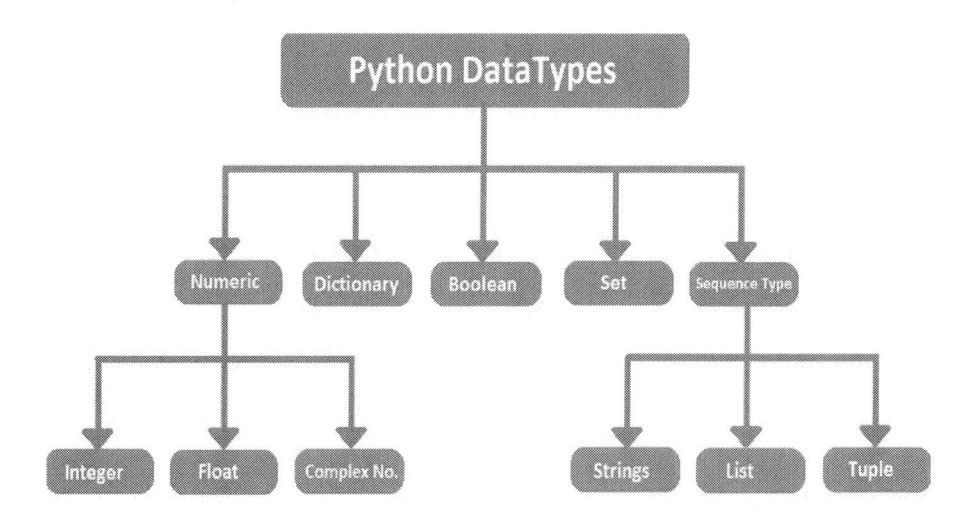

Background

Think about the numerous kinds of data we encounter daily as a starting point for thinking about data types. Numbers are an example of data in the real world: we can use entire numbers (0, 1, 2,), integers (..., -1, 0, 1,), and irrational numbers () as examples of data in the real world. In mathematics, we can mix numbers of different types to arrive at some solution most of the time. We might even want to add five to the end of a number, as five plus one equals ten. It is possible to leave the equation also as an answer in account for a said irrational number, or we can round to a value with a limited number of digits and then add those numbers together. The situation becomes more complicated if we attempt to assess numbers using other data, such as words, as we have done here. What method would we use to solve the following equation?

Sky + 8 is a mathematical expression.

For computers, every data type, such as words and numbers, can be conceived of as different from the others, so we must be cautious about how we assign values to them and alter them through operations.

2.1: Mutable Data Type

Word "Mutable" indicates that the underlying state of an item can be modified or mutated in some way. As a result, the most straightforward definition is: A mutable object is one whose internal information can be altered. On the other hand, immutable objects do not allow any changes to be made after they have been formed. In Python, a variable can be defined as an object that can change or be treated as something that can change naturally. The capacity to modify and edit a value is referred to as mutability. Mutable classes in Python allow programmers to create objects that can have their values changed at any time. They are typically used to store a large amount of data in one location. When anything mutates, the integral controller applicable within an item change. It is referred to as "mutational transformation." Lists, sets, and dictionaries are examples of mutable built-in types. User-

Defined Classes are another mutable built-in type. Defining the attributes is entirely up to the user when defining the attributes.

Lists are like dynamically sized arrays, which can be declared in another language, except that they are smaller. Lists are changeable, meaning they can be changed even after being created. Lists in Python are sorted and have a specific number of items. Indexing is done in a list by starting with the number zero and working your way up to the highest number in the list, and so on. Each element has a clear location, thus allowing for duplication of elements in the array, with each member having its distinctive position and credibility in the list.

2.2: List in Python

Lists can be built-in Python by simply putting the series of characters within the square brackets[]. In contrast to Sets, the generation of a list does not necessitate the use of a built-in function. The list is a term used to refer to an organized sequence of elements. In Python, it is a data type that is extremely versatile. All of the values inside the list don't need to have the same type of data as the values in the previous list. The List data type is one of the most frequently used data types in the Python programming language. The list datatype in Python is the unique datatype for storing data that may be used in various ways. Python can hold a variety of various sorts of data with relative ease. Declaring a list is straightforward. The list was enclosed in brackets, and commas are used to

distinguish between the things on the list. A list can be represented as follows: >>> a = [5,9.9,'list']. It is also possible to change an entry number in the list.

2.3: Python Sets

Set is a compilation of one-of-a-kind items not arranged in any sequence. Braces denote a specified set, and a comma has been used to denote the separation of values. Inside a set data type, one will discover that the pieces are not in any sequence. Duplicate values are deleted in a set, which only retains unique values. Intersection and union are operations that can be done on two sets of data. A set is a group of elements not in any sequence.

On the other hand, a set is malleable in and of itself. We can add or remove things from it. Sets can also be used to conduct mathematical set operations such as union, intersect, symmetric difference, and other similar operations on a collection of items. A key to the success of set-in mathematics might be esoteric and hard to grasp at first glance. Compared to other object types, sets are distinguished by the number of distinct operations that may be done on them.

Creating Python Sets

A variety of items of varying categories can be included in any number of items.

Example Code

my_set = {1, 10, 3, 4, 3, 2}

#set has been initialized

print(my_set)

my_set = set([1, 10, 3, 2])

print(my_set)

my_set = {1, 10, [3, 4]}

2.4: Dictionary In Python

Dictionary in Python is a random collection of data values that can be used to store data values like a map. However, unlike some other Data Types that can only carry a data point as an element, Dictionary can hold a key: value pair and a single value. Both dictionaries and lists share the following features:

- Both are malleable, and both are dynamic.
- They can grow and decrease as needed.
- They can both be nested. A list can include another list and vice versa.

Depending on the context, a dictionary could also prepare a set and vice versa. The primary difference between dictionaries and lists is how elements are accessed: list elements may be retrieved based on their place in the list, whereas dictionary elements can be accessed based on their keys.

Creating A Dictionary In Python

A dictionary can be created by simply putting things inside curly brackets and separating them with commas, as seen below. An item does indeed have a key and just a corresponding value, which is both stated as a pair of numbers (Key: value). However, while the values could be of data type and can be repeated, the keys must be of an immutable data type (a string, number, or tuple containing immutable elements) and should be distinct. It is possible to create a Dictionary in Python by enclosing a sequence of objects within curly braces and separating them with the character 'comma.' Dictionary contains pairs of values, one of which is the Key, and the other is the corresponding pair element, the Key: value pair. When using a dictionary, values could have been of data type and copied, whereas keys cannot be duplicated and should be immutable. Values can be of any data and can be duplicated.

Adding Elements To The Dictionary

A Dictionary is being expanded by adding new elements. The insertion of elements in a Python dictionary can be accomplished in various ways. A single value can be created to a Dictionary at a time by declaring the value together with the Key, for example, Dict[Key] = 'Value.' Using the Dictionary's built-in update() method, you can change an existing value in the Dictionary. Key values nested within each other can even be added to the current Dictionary.

2.5: Immutable Data Types

Data types that are immutable differ from the mutable siblings in that they cannot be modified after they have been created.

Numeric data types, characters, bytes, sets, and multivalued are all examples of immutable types, as are numeric data types. There are numerous uses for immutability in various sensitive jobs that we perform in a network-centric environment when we allow for parallelization. Making immutable objects allows you to protect the values and guarantee that no other threads can alter or update your stored data. It is also useful in instances where you want to produce a bit of code that could be changed in any way after it has been written. Debug code that tried to discover the value of such an immutable object, for example, is an example. As defined by the Python documentation, immutable structures in Python are objects whose values and properties do not change over time.

Following their creation and initialization, these objects become permanent, and they are an essential component of the data structures in Python. Python is utilized in integers, tuples, characters, frozen sets, or user-defined classes with a few exceptions. They cannot be changed, and their values and state remain constant once they have been initialized, so they are referred to as immutable.

1. Numeric
2. String

3. Tuple

2.6: Numeric Data Types

Previously, you learned about the immutability of integers; similarly, Python's other built-in integer data types, such as Booleans, floating, real, or complex, fractions, and decimals, are also impervious to mutations and changes. Python's textual data is managed via str objects, also known as strings in common parlance. They are sequences containing Unicode code points that cannot be changed. A set of Unicode code points can represent a character. Although textual data can be stored and transmitted on a network, it is often necessary to encode it to make it compatible with the medium it will be transmitted. If you encode something with bytes, you get something that looks and behaves like a string, but it has a different syntax and behavior.

In Python, floating-point numbers are defined as floats, whereas integers are defined as ints. Among the types of data types included in this category are lengthy datatypes, which are as follows: It is used to store integers that are longer than a certain length. This datatype was only available in Python 2. x, and it was later removed from the language in Python 3. x. The "Type()" method determines the type of value or variable referenced. The "isinstance()" function determines whether or not a given class has a value. The number of an integer has no upper limit in its size. Integers of any length are permitted without restriction, and they can be as large as the greatest amount of system memory that is accessible. Number with Floating Points, The distinction between floating-point and integers is the presence or absence of decimal places. A floating-point integer can indeed be represented by the symbol "1.0," whereas an integer can also be represented by the symbol "1. It has a precision of up to Fifteen decimal points. The writing system of the real or complex is "x + yj," which stands for "x plus yj." Here, y represents the imaginary component of the equation, and x represents the real part of the equation.

2.7: Tuple

A tuple is a type in Python that represents an organized collection of objects, similar to a list. The way people pronounce things differs depending on who you ask. Some people say it as if it were spelled "too-ple" (rhyming with "Mott the Hoople"). My preference is for the latter because it is presumed to originate from the same root as the words "quintuple," "sextuple," "octuple," and so on and because everyone I know enunciates these latter words as though to rhyme with the word "supply."

Tuples are similar to the list in all ways, except for the following characteristics:

- Tuples are defined by surrounding the components in parentheses (()) rather than square brackets, as in the following example: ([]).
- Tuples are immutable in nature.

Here's a quick example of a tuple declaration, indexing, and slicing from which you can learn.

Benefit Of Using A Tuple

- Program performance is significantly faster than manipulating an equivalent List when manipulating a tuple.
- There are occasions when you don't want the information to be changed.
- If the values inside the collection are intended to move at a constant for the duration of the program, using a tuple rather than a list prevents accidental modification.
- There's also another Python data type, called a dictionary that you should encounter shortly and which necessitates one of its elements, a value of an immutable

type. Tuples are permitted for this purpose, while lists are not permitted.

Rule Of Immutability

There are exceptions to the immutability rule in Python, just as in any other language. Not all immutable things have the property of being malleable. It will cause a great deal of uncertainty in your head. Let us use an example to better comprehend what we are talking about. Take, for example, a tuple 'tup.' Consider the tuple tup = ('GreatLearning,' [4,3,1,2]); we can observe that the tuple contains elements of several data types, as seen in the following example. The first entry in this array is a string, which cannot be changed since we all know it. As we mentioned earlier, the second component is a list, which we all knew is mutable. We are all aware that a tuple is an immutable type of data in and of itself. It is unable to alter the contents of the file. However, the list contained within it can change its contents. As a result, while the value of Immutable objects could be modified, the values of their constituent objects can. Change the value of the variable.

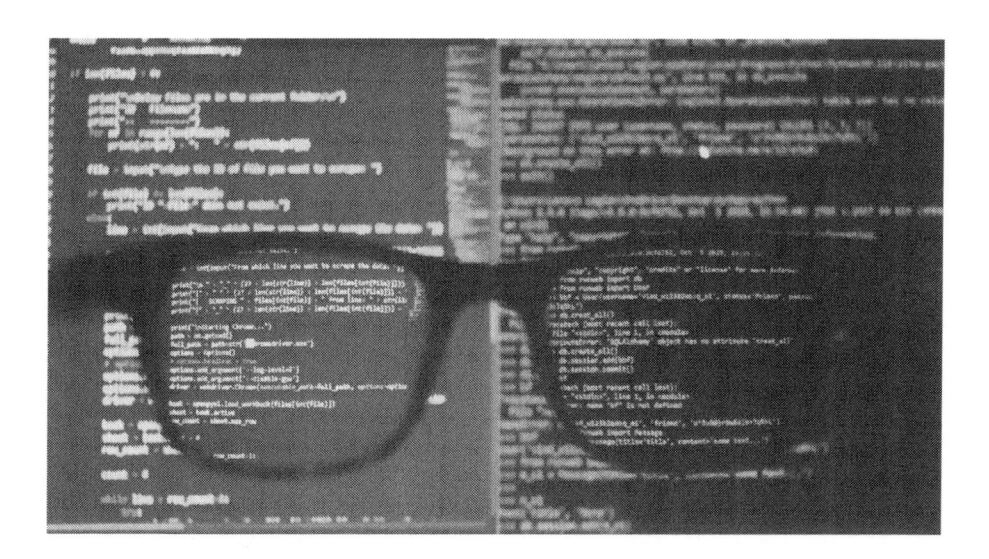

Creating A Tuple

A tuple is formed by enclosing all the items (elements) within parenthesis () and separating them with commas (). The use of parenthesis is entirely optional. Using them, on the other hand, is a good practice. A tuple can contain any number of elements, and they can be of any type and size.

Example Code

tuple = ()

print(tuple)

tuple = (1, 2, 3)

print(tuple)

tuple = (1, "Hello", 3.4)

print(tuple)

tuple = ("cat", [8, 4, 6], (1, 2, 3))

print(tuple)

Every computer language is based on core elements that form the framework for the language. In Python programming, these basic constituents are referred to as data types. Python contains a built-in type of data that provides insight into the values stored in each data structure. They specify which actions can be done on a specific piece of data and how the programming flow should be implemented.

String

Strings comprise arrays of bytes representing the Unicode characters in the Python programming language. The character data type in Python does not exist, and a character is merely a string with the length of one in Python. Accessing elements of a string can be accomplished by using square brackets.

Chapter 3: Loops and Conditional Statements

Statements & loops are the building blocks of Python programming, and they constitute the whole language. Procedures, statements, methods, & loops are all mentioned in this section, and they are all essential in the development of a good Python program. For the inclusion of operation runners in Python programming language's libraries, there are a variety of justifications for doing so. This section will examine/discuss the applicability of these programs and their characteristics.

3.1: Conditional Programming

The phrase "control of flow" refers to the chronological sequence of statements that are processed in the program and is defined as follows: All the curricula/programs that we have looked at so far have a straightforward control flow: the instructions are executed one by one in the order that they are specified. In most cases, the structure of a program is more intricate, with statements that may or may not be performed based on circumstances (conditionals) or groupings of statements that are run many times (loops).

If else statement

Most calculations need distinct actions depending on the inputs. Flip.py is a Python program that writes the outcomes of a coin flip using an if-else statement. The table below outlines some common scenarios where you may need to utilize an if or an if-else statement in your programming.

absolute value	`if x < 0:` `    x = -x`

put x and y into sorted order	`if x > y:`
	`    temp = x`
	`    x = y`
	`    y = temp`

maximum of x and y	`if x > y: maximum = x` `else:     maximum = y`
error check for remainder operation	`if den == 0: stdio.writeln('Division by zero')` `else:        stdio.writeln('Remainder = ' + num % den)`

error check for quadratic formula	`discriminant = b*b - 4.0*a*c`
	`if discriminant < 0.0:`
	`    stdio.writeln('No real roots')`
	`else:`
	`    d = math.sqrt(discriminant)`
	`    stdio.writeln((-b + d)/2.0)`
	`    stdio.writeln((-b - d)/2.0)`

In real life, there are moments when we must make specific judgments and then figure out what to do next established/based on the results of those decisions. Similar situations arise in programming because we must make certain choices and then execute the next code block because of those decisions. Decision-making statements are used in programming languages to decide the direction in which program execution will continue. The if-else statement is used in Python to make judgments. The other statement is characterized as a switch statement combined with an if statement. If the condition statement in the if-statement settles to something like a value of 0 or a FALSE value will be included in another statement, the code is run.

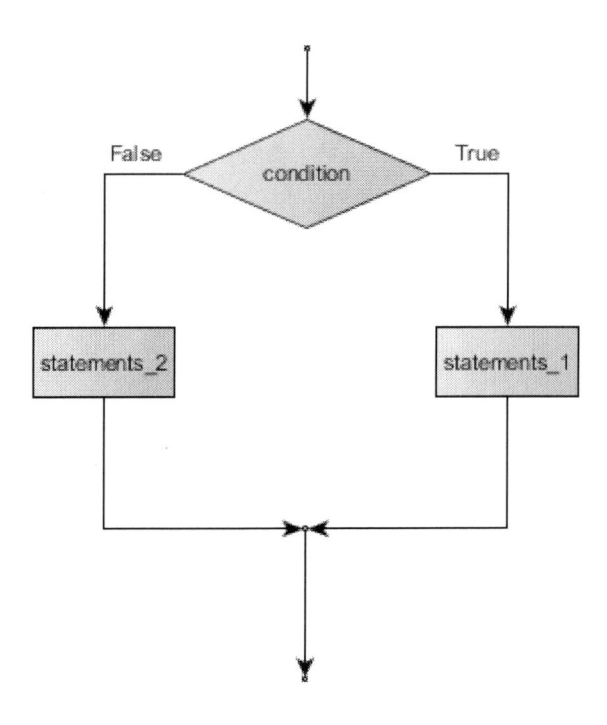

The other statement is optional, and following the if statement, there can only be one else statement. Python supports the following conditions

1. **Equals** a == b

2. **Not Equal** a! = b

3. **Less than** a < b

4. **Less than or equal to** a <= b

5. **Greater than**: a > b

6. **Greater than or equal to** a >= b

Syntax

if expression:

   statements

else:

   statements

Code

#print a message according to code

number = 10

if number > 0:

   print(number, "Positive number.")

print("Always Printed.")

num = -2

if num > 0:

   print(num, " Negative number.")

For example, the test phase above is numeric greater than zero (numerical greater than zero). Suppose the result of these expressions is True; the rest of the if statement is conducted. Whenever the value of the variable num matches three, the test expression evaluates to true, and all the statements included inside the body of the if statement is executed. If the variable number is greater than or equal to -3, the expression is false, and the statements within/inside the body of the if statement is not executed. The print() instruction falls outside the if condition's scope (unintended). It results in the program being executed regardless of the value of the testing expression.

It is important to note that in Python, indentation has significance. Consider the following two code segments, for example

if x >= 0:

   stdio.write('NOT ')

stdio.writeln('NEGATIVE')

if x >= 0:

 stdio.write('NOT ')

stdio.writeln('NEGATIVE')

For any x value higher than or equal to 0, the words "not negative" appear in both pieces of the sentence. For example, if x is less than zero, the upper code prints 'negative', while the lower code prints nothing.

If-Elif-Else

A block of code or a piece of code might be executed as soon as possible. The statement of Leif evaluates a single condition to TRUE, allowing you to check numerous expressions for TRUE at the same time with the same phrase. In the same manner that the otherwise statement is not required, the if statement also isn't required. Instead of just having one Elif statement after such an if, as is the case with somebody, there is no limit to the number of Elif statements that may be used after an if in this situation.

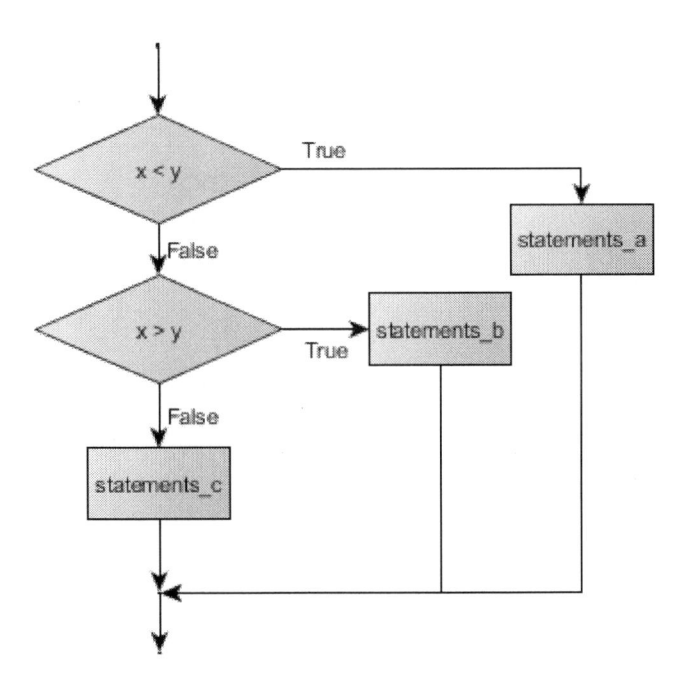

The If-Else-statement Elif's may be used to execute any single statement or even a block of statements only if and only if specific criteria are matched. Conditions may be either true or false; whenever a condition is true, some(one) action is done, and when a condition is false, another action is performed; conditions can be either true or false.

Syntax

if expression (1):

   statements

elif expression (2):

   statements

elif expression (3):

   statements

else:

   statements

Example Code

var = 50

if var == 100:

   print "1 – You've got expression true value"

   print var

elif var == 130:

    print "2 – You've got expression true value"

    print var

elif var == 50:

    print "3 – You've got expression true value"

    print var

else:

    print "4 – You've got false expression value."

    print var

#Now, Print the message before terminating the program

print "Have a Nice Day!!!"

Nested If Statements

When an If-Else-Elif statement is included inside another If-Else-Elif statement, the outcome is the same as when the statements are not contained within each other. It is referred to as layering in the context of computer programming. It is conceivable to stack any number of these statements on top of one another inside a single statement. When determining the nesting level, the only way available is to look just at the indentation. They may be difficult to comprehend. Because of this, they should indeed be avoided until the IF functions necessarily have a test with just two potential outcomes: TRUE / FALSE. There have been no IF functions in programming. Because nested IF functions, which are defined as one IF function inside another, allow you to evaluate many criteria simultaneously and therefore increase the number of outcomes, these are often used in simulations to assess multiple criteria simultaneously. According to the performance on the exam, we would want to assign a grade to each of the students. As a result, nested If Statements are used in various computer languages.

If, while, and for statements can be nested in comparison if, while, and for statements, and vice versa; in the file divisorpattern.py, for example, there is a for loop with nested statements that are another for loop (where a nested statement is indeed an if statement) and the statement stdio.writeln().

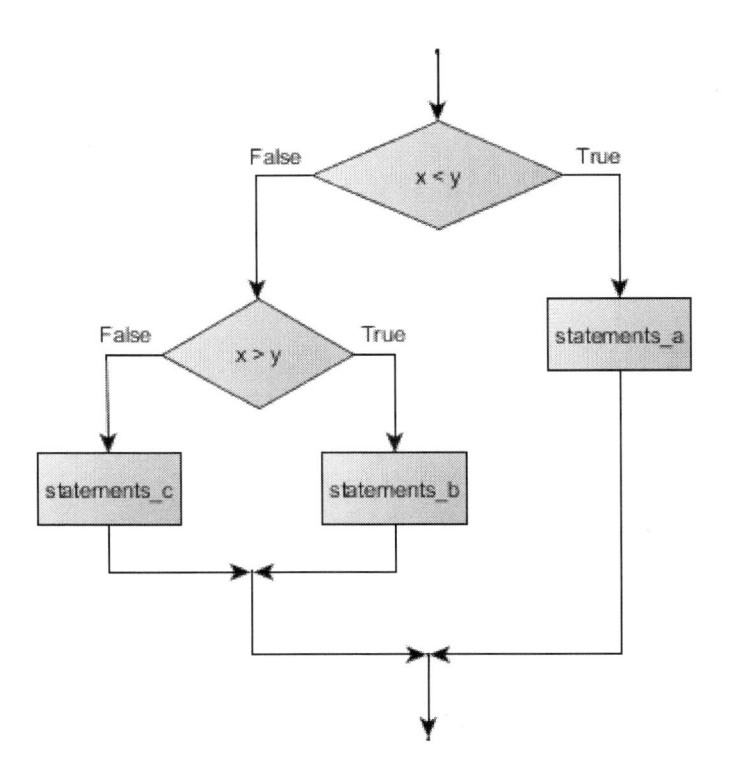

Two branches are included inside the outer conditional. The second branch still has another one if statement, which contains two other branches. Conditional statements might be included in any of the two branches as well. Even though the structure is obvious due to the indentation of a statement, nested conditionals rapidly become difficult to comprehend. In general, it's a good reason to stay away from them if possible. Logical operators are often used to simplify conditional statements that are nested inside one another.

Syntax

if(condition):

   statements

if(condition):

   statements

else:

Code

```
#Program to show nested If statement
i = 50
if (i == 50):
    # First if statement
    if (i < 100):
        print ("i is smaller as compared to 100")
    # Nested - if statement
    if (i < 70):
        print ("i is smaller as compared to 70 too")
    else:
        print ("i is greater as compared to 100")
```

Iteration

Computers are frequently used to automate the completion of monotonous activities. Performing the same or comparable activities repeatedly without making mistakes is something that computers excel at and humans struggle with. Iteration is the word/term used to describe the repeated execution of such a sequence of statements. Python contains two statements for iteration.

3.2: Loops

In general, assertions are executed in the order they are received. There are, however, certain exceptions. You may need to execute a piece of code numerous times in different situations. Several control structures are available in programming languages, which allow for the implementation of more sophisticated execution pathways. A loop statement allows us to repeatedly run a statement or set of statements.

For Loop

With for loop in Python, it is feasible to iterate over a sequence (list, tuple, or string) or other iterable objects. Traversal is the term used to describe the process of iterating through a sequence. The loop variable is used to run a set of statements several times and compress the code that manages the loop variable to a small amount of space. It operates in an indefinite while loop until the Stop Iteration signal is received, at which point it terminates. It is necessary to retrieve the next element in the fruits array using the next() function during the attempted block.

Iterating through a structure/system is done using a for loop (a tuple, a list, the dictionary, a string, or a set). It is like an iterator process seen in other OOP (object-oriented programming) languages than for keywords in those other programming computer languages.

The for loop collaborates with Python's sequence data types, such as strings, lists, and tuples, to process each item in a sequence. The loop body is run after each item is (re-)assigned to a loop variable.

Syntax

for VARIABLE in sequence:

   Statements

It is just another example of such a compound statement for Python, & it includes a header that ends in a colon (:) and a body that consists of a series with one or even more statements indented the same amount from the header the branching statements. You don't need to construct the loop variable before first for statement runs since it is generated whenever for statement runs. The loop variable is assigned to the next element within the sequence with each iteration, and the body statements are then executed. When the final element within the sequence is reached, the statement ends. This flowing form is termed a loop because it loops straight to the start after each iteration.

Code

print ("Here List Iteration")

2 = ["Cats", "or" " Dogs "]

For i in 2:

    print(i)

Iterating over a tuple (immutable)

print ("\nHere Tuple Iteration")

t = ("Cat", "or" "Dogs")

For i in U:

    print(i)

print ("\nHere String Iteration")

```
s = "Mice"

For i in s:

    print(i)

print ("\nHence Dictionary Iteration")

d = dict ()

d['xyz'] = 321

d['abc'] = 543

For i in d:

    print ("%s %d" % (i, d[i]))
```

For Loop with Else

An additional box can be employed when using a for a loop. The else section is executed if the items in the sequence used in for loop are exhausted. It is sufficient to split a for a loop by using a broken keyword. In this case, the other portion is not considered. Therefore, the for loop is run in the else section if no break occurs.

While Statement

Many calculations are, by their very nature, repetitious. The while statement allows us to repeat a set of statements multiple times. It allows us to express complex calculations without writing a lot of code. Ten times, the program tenhellos.py writes "Hello, World." The command-line input n is sent to the program powersoftwo.py, which outputs all powers of two or less than equal to n.

In Python, we may use the normal approximation I += 1 to shorten an assignment's statement of the type I = I + 1. Other binary operators, such as -, *, and /, use the same notation. In powersoftwo.py, for example, many programmers would be using power *= 2 rather than power = 2 * power.

Syntax

while expression:

    statements

While Loop and Else

If the condition inside while loop condition turns False, the else section of the program is performed. A break statement could bring the while loop to an end. In such instances, the other portion is not considered. Therefore, if, unhappily, no break arises and consequently condition is false, an else section a while loop is run.

Chapter 4: Python Functions

In programming, functions are used to group a collection of instructions that you wish to use again or that, due to complexity, are better confined in a semi and called only when required. In other words, a function is indeed a block of software that is created to do a certain goal. The function may or may not need several inputs to complete the particular job. Depending on the circumstances, the function may or may not return any or more values when the work is completed.

Suppose you are familiar with the Python programming language. In that case, you may have already experienced and used some of the numerous fantastic features that are built-in to the Python language or included with its library ecosystem. Functions are an important component of the Python language. As a Data Science, you will, on the other hand, be required to create your functions regularly to tackle the difficulties that your data present to you.

You may have already utilized some of the great functions provided by the Python programming language or its library environment; functions are an essential component of the Python programming language. As a Data Scientist, on the other hand, you'll be asked to construct your functions regularly to solve the problems that your data provides. Functions are chunks of code that may be reused and organized so that they execute a single, related action. Functions increase the modularity of your program and allow you to recover a significant amount of code space. In addition to the built-in methods such as print() that Python provides, you may create your functions using the Python programming language. They're referred to as "user-defined functions" in this context.

To build a procedure in Python, follow these basic instructions. The word def is preceded by the function's name in a function block, followed by parentheses (()). Any input or arguments should be included inside this parenthesis. You might additionally specify parameters inside this parenthesis if necessary. The documentation language of the function, often known as the docstring, may be included as an additional statement in the function's first statement. Every function's code starts with a semicolon (:), and as a result, the code block is compressed. When it comes to coding, functions are quite crucial. Their objective is to break down enormous programs into manageable chunks of time. In the parentheses, you will find the unique pieces of code that are included inside them. In addition, a function is given a name. They provide a variety of functions. They are cast off from courses to fill certain jobs.

Python Functions as well as the Importance of Their Use

The following are some of the most significant advantages of Python functions:

- It is used to prevent reusing the same code over and again. Thanks to the function, everything may be made functional with a single code, which allows the developer to save a significant amount of time.

- Reusability is among the most important characteristics, and it makes it much simpler for users since the block of code may be used anywhere inside the application.

- The features allow us to deal with large-scale projects. Developers often use functions to split collaboration among them.

4.1: Using Functions and their Return Values

Python is a computer language that has a large number of functions. They may be invoked from the translator package and used to deploy to any application that is supported by it. The software community is uninterested in this language for the time being. Today, they are used all around the globe to do all of the primary programming jobs associated with data science and several other initiatives.

1. The Difference Between Functions And Methods

When a function is included inside a class, it is considered a process. It is accessed via standards for different objects. This constraint does not apply to a group function; rather, it applies to a solo performance. It emphasizes that, although all methods were functional, not all functions were methods in the same sense that all methods were functions. For example, suppose you first write the plus() method and then create a Summarizing class that has a sum() method of the same name:

Example Code

Define a function

def plus(a,b):

return a + b

Create a `Sum` class

class Sum (object):

def sum(self, a, b):

self.contents = a + b

return self.contents

2. The Difference Between Parameters and Arguments

When functions and methods are created and mapped arguments, they are given the names of the parameters. When calling a function or procedure, arguments appear to be the items provided in the function or process call, although the function or encoding refers to the arguments by their names as parameters. Consider the following situation, and then go to the DataCamp Light portion of the website: Even though you provided three arguments, self, a, then b, you only supply two variables to the sum() function of the Summation class. Whenever a class method takes the first argument, that argument is always related to the class's current context, which in this case is Summation. The term "self" is widely used to refer to this argument. In this circumstance, it is unnecessary to send references to oneself since self is the variable's identifier for just an implicitly supplied argument associated with the instance through which a method is executed. It is implicitly included in the discussion via the use of an example.

3. Passing by reference as opposed to passing by value

Python is a computer language in which all variables

(arguments) are given by reference rather than sent directly. It implies that if you change the values of parameters inside a function, the change is reflected in the call to the function.

4.2: Recursive Function

Those acquainted with Python's functions will know that it is fairly usual for one procedure to call another. Python allows functions to call themselves as well as other functions. In programming language terms, a recursive function can be expressed as one that calls itself, and the method of utilizing such recursive functions is defined as recursive programming.

A function calling may initially appear strange, but recursively, many programming issues are better described, as seen in the following example. When you come up against an issue like this, recursion is invaluable in your arsenal of tools and techniques.

When the defined word occurs, this is referred to as a recursive definition. Self-referential situations often arise in everyday life, even if they aren't immediately apparent as being self-referential. Consider the following scenario: you wished to explain the group of individuals that comprised your ancestors.

The majority of programming issues may be solved without the use of recursion. As a result, recursion isn't always required, at least technically speaking.

Although certain instances, such as the definition of ancestors mentioned above, lend themselves extremely well to a self-referential definition, others do not. If you were designing an algorithm to deal with such a problem programmatically, a recursion solution would be clearer and more concise than a non-recursive approach in this instance.

Another interesting example is the traversal of data structures similar to trees. Because they are layered structures, they easily conform to the notion of a recursive structure. A non-recursive technique for traversing a hierarchical structure was likely clumsy, while a recursive approach is elegant.

Python's interpreter establishes a new local domain when you call a function. It prevents names specified inside that function from colliding with names defined elsewhere. One function may call another, and although they both declare objects with much the same name, everything works out perfectly since the objects in question reside in distinct namespaces so that they can be called from the same function.

The same is true if more than one instance of the same function is executing simultaneously in parallel. Consider the following definition, for instance:

Example Code

def rec_function():

   x = 15

   rec_function()

Upon the first execution of the function(), Python constructs a namespace and then assigns the value 15 to the variable x in that namespace. Then function() runs itself a second time, and so on. The interpreter generates a second domain and assigns the value 15 to x in that namespace. But they're in different namespaces; these two occurrences of the term x were distinct and may survive without interfering.

Chapter 5: Object-Oriented Programming In Python

Programming with object-oriented principles is a programming model which allows you to organize programs so that attributes and behaviors are grouped in individual objects rather than in the program itself. For example, a person could be represented by an object with properties such as a name, age, address, and behaviors such as walking, speaking, breathing, and running. Alternatively, it might represent an email with features such as a list, subject, body, and behaviors such as attaching files and sending the email. Item programming is a method of modeling physical, real-world objects, such as automobiles, and relationships between objects, such as between employees and businesses, students, professors, etc.

Real-world entities are represented as software objects in object-oriented programming (OOP), which have certain data associated with all of them and can execute specific actions. In addition to procedural programming, which arranges a program like a recipe in that it gives a set of stages, in the form of function and modifications, that stream sequentially to accomplish tasks, another standard programming paradigm is object-oriented programming. The most important lesson is that objects are at the heart of object-oriented programming, serving not only as data representations, as they do in structured programming but also as structural elements of the program.

5.1: Python Class

A class is a blueprint or prototype defined by the user and from which objects are produced. Classes are a convenient way of grouping network services together in a single place. Creating a new class creates a new specific object, which allows for creating training examples of that type. Each instance of a class can have attributes linked to it to keep track of its current state. Class instances can also contain methods for affecting the state of the object they reside.

Consider the following scenario: you wanted to count the

number of dogs of various breeds and ages, and you wanted to count the number of dogs of each breed and age. The first element may be the dog's breed, and the second factor could be the dog's age if the latter is desired. Consider the following scenario: there are one hundred different dogs. How would you determine which element is meant to belong to which? What if we wanted to give these dogs some additional characteristics? It is an example of a lack of organization required for classes. A class creates a consumer data structure with its data and functions and member methods, which can be read and used by establishing a class instance. A class instance can be read and used by any other class instance. A class can be thought of as a blueprint for an object. Basic data structures such as numbers, phrases, and lists are expected to describe simple data such as the price of an apple, the title of a poem, or the colors of your favorite shirt, among other things. How do you go about it if you want to portray something more complex? Consider the following scenario: you want to keep track of all of the employees in your company. Basic information about every person, including their name, age, job title, and the year they began working, must be kept on record. One method of accomplishing this is to express each worker as a list as follows:

5.2: Classes And Instances

Class is used to generate data structures that are specific to the user. Classes define functions known as methods, which indicate the behaviors and actions an object generated from the class can execute with its data. Methods are defined by the data stored in the object produced from the class. The Dog class will be created in this lesson, which will contain information about the features and behaviors that a particular dog may exhibit. A class is a template for how something will be defined in a programming language. It does not contain any information. When establishing a dog, the Dog class stipulates that it is important to include a surname and an age; yet it does not include the name and age of any particular dog. Whereas a class is a blueprint for creating objects, and instances is an entity constructed from a type and contains actual data. An instance of a Dog type is no longer considered a blueprint. It's a real dog with just a name, such as Miles, who is four years old and lives in a house.

To put it differently, a class is analogous to a form or a survey. An instance can be regarded as a type that has already been filled with relevant information. In the same way that many users can fill out the same form according to their metadata, multiple instances of a single class can be placed in a single class.

5.3: Inherit From Other Classes in Python

Taking on the properties and behaviors of another class is the process through which one class gains the properties and behaviors. Classes that are newly formed are referred to as child classes, and classes from which child classes are generated are referred to as parent classes. A child class's attributes and methods can be overridden or extended the same way as parent classes. In other terms, child classes inherit all the properties and methods of their parent classes, but they can also provide properties and behaviors specific to themselves. Object inheritance can be thought akin to genetic inheritance, despite the comparison being not perfect. It's a characteristic with which you were born. Consider the following scenario: you wish to dye your hair purple. You've just successfully overridden the trait of having purple hair that you acquired from your mother, assuming she doesn't have purple hair herself.

5.4: Variables in Python

During the execution of a computer program, variables have been used to store data that can be referenced and updated. We can also use them to label data with such a descriptive name, making our program easier to read for both the user and us. Variables could be regarded as data storage containers that hold information. They exist solely to categorize and store data in memory. This data can then be utilized in other areas of your software to improve its overall performance. In Python, a variable is a memory space that has been designated for storing values. In other words, a variable inside a Python program contains information that the computer can use to do calculations.

In Python, every value represented by a datatypPython supports various data types, including lists, numbers, tuples, strings, dictionaries, etc. In Python, variables can be named anything. Identifying and naming variables is one of the most demanding and tough processes in computer programming. When naming variables, it is important to think about the names thoroughly. Please make every effort to verify that the description you give to your variable is exact and understandable to a serial device before using it. Occasionally, when you revisit a program that you wrote months or even years ago, you may discover that the other reader is none other than yourself. Python is not a fixed programming language in the traditional sense. Before using variables, we do not need to define them or specify their kinds. When we first assign a variable value, we refer to this as "creating" the variable. A variable is a name assigned to a memory region to distinguish it from other memory locations. It serves as the fundamental storage unit for a program.

When an expression checks variables, you can save the result and utilize it later. Variables can be thought of as a box that can hold information.

In Python, you can declare a variable.

When a variable is given an input statement, it is instructed to store a value. Type the name of the variable first, followed either by the = sign (also called the opcode) and then the value that will be put in the variable. For example, you may put spam = 100 into the interactive shell. The value of a variable can be

changed while the program is still running. A constant is nothing but a name for a location in memory; anything you can do with it affects location in memory.

Example Code

Num = 50

print(Num)

Declare Different Types Of Variables In Python

The most often used variables in Python are integers, long integers, floats, or string variables.

1. Integer Integers are used to represent numeric quantities in computer programs.

2. Integer with a long tail

3. It is possible to have an integer type variable with a length more than a conventional integer type variable.

4. Float Variables are variables used to hold precession data that are in a state of constant motion.

Variable Casting In Python

Variable costing is a term used to describe converting a variable from one type to another. The casting functions oversee changing variables from their early form to their new representation in the new representation.

To convert a to a standard integer, use the int function (a).

To convert a to a large integer, use the long function (a).

To convert a to point value, use the float command (a).

Code:

A = int(10)

B = int(20.0)

C = int("30")

5.5: Polymorphism in Python

In Python, polymorphism refers to an object's ability to take on various forms. In plain language, polymorphism is the ability to do the same task in distinct ways. While at work, for example, Jessa assumes an employee's role. And she's at home; on the other hand, she behaves more like a wife. She also shows herself in various ways, depending on where she is. As a result, the same person appears differently depending on the situation. The built-in function len exhibits polymorphism (). The constructed function len() estimates the tape measure based on the kind of object being calculated. When given a string as an argument, this function returns the number of characters in the string, and when given an array as an argument, this function gives the number of elements in an array. The len() technique considers an object according to the type of the item's class.

Polymorphism With Inheritance

Most of the time, polymorphism is utilized in conjunction with inheritance. In inheritance, the attributes of the methods of a base class are passed down to the child class. In programming, a base class or class label is the existing class, while the new class is a subclass, child class, or derived class. It is possible to define methods in the child class and have the same name as methods in the parent class by utilizing method overriding polymorphism. This process is known as Method Overriding, and this process is an inherited method in a child class performed in the parent class.

The advantage of overriding methods

- It is useful when we wish to increase the functionality of a method by making changes to the inherited method. Sometimes a method inheriting from a parent class does not meet the needs of a subclass; in this case, we need to completely redo the parent class function in the subclass, using a different approach.

- It is handy that whenever a parent class contains numerous child classes, one of those child classes wants to redefine a method in the parent class. The other child classes can use the method of the parent class. Consequently, we do not need to change the parent class code. When we call a polymorphism method, the Programming language first validates the object's class type and then performs the appropriate method based on the class type. For instance, if you construct a Car object, Python will execute the speed() function from the Car class when the object is created. Overriding the Method. In this instance, we get a vehicle class that serves as a parent class, with subclasses such as 'Car' and 'Truck.' In contrast, because each car may differ in terms of seating capacity, speed, and so on, we could have the same example method in each class while having a completely distinct implementation in each class.

5.6: Python's Operator Overloading

For example, adding two integers, joining two strings, and merging two lists are all possible with the operation +. It is possible because the '+' operator was overloaded by the int and str classes. If the same built-in operators or function behaves when applied to objects of various classes, this is Operator Overloading in the programming language.

It results in an error since the compiler does not understand how to add two things together. Thus, we create a function for an operator, operator overloading in this case. We have the ability to overload all existing operators, but we are unable to establish a new operator. Operational overloading is accomplished by using special or magic functions provided by Python, which are automatically invoked when associated with a certain operator. When we use the + operator, for example, the secret method __add__ is immediately invoked, which defines the operation for the + operator.

When we employ an operator on a user-defined data type, the system automatically invokes a special operation or magic some in with all of that operator. Making an operator behave differently from a method or function is as simple as making them behave differently. Methods are declared in your class, and operators operate according to the method definitions' behavior. When we use the + operator, the mystical method __add__ is immediately invoked, which defines the operation for the + operator. By altering the code of this magic procedure, we may give the + operator a new and more meaningful meaning.

Chapter 6: List and Built-in Functions

6.1: Lists

We'll study everything about Python lists with the assistance of examples.

len()

The Python list function len() returns the exact size(number of elements) of the list by invoking the list object's native length function. It takes inside a list object as a parameter but does have the side effect just on the list.

Syntax

len(s)

Wheres might be a sequence and otherwise collection.

Code

Function which computes & returns the length(size) of a list.

```
def get_len(l):
    # Python len() list function computes length of list.
    return len(l)
if __name__ == '__main__':
    l1 = []           # empty list defined
```

```
l20 = [50,430,60,10]       # 4 elements list defined

l30 = [[40,30],[00,10],[30]]   # 3 elements(lists) defined

print("1 length: ", get_len(l10))

print("2 length: ", get_len(l20))

print("3 length: ", get_len(l30))
```

list()

List () is a Python built-in method that constructs a list of an iterable supplied as an argument. Since it will be used frequently during this session, we will briefly examine what this class provides.

Syntax

list([iterable])

The bracket notifies us that the argument supplied to it is negotiable.

The list() method is usually used to

- Convert various sequences as well as iterables to the list.
- Generate an empty list — No parameter is passed to the function in this situation.

range()

range() is a Python list function that accepts a list of integers as an argument and returns a list of numbers.

Syntax

range([start,]stop[,step])

Here

- start: Indicates where the list's integer generation should begin.
- Stop: Indicates when the list should stop producing integers.
- Step Indicates how many times the value will be incremented.

Start & step both are optional in the syntax above, and they equate to zero & one, respectively.

The sum() method in Python sums all the elements in an iterable & returns the total.

Syntax

sum(iterable[,start])

Here:

- From left to right, the iterable includes objects to be added.

- The start is a positive integer which will be appended to the value returned.

The items and the start of the iterable should both be integers. If no value is specified for a start, it resets to zero (0).

min()

The Python min() method returns the first item in such a sequence that is the smallest.

Syntax

minimum (iterable[,key, default])

Here

- A list of objects will be iterable here.
- The key defines a single-argument function for extracting a comparison keyword from every list member.
- If iterable is empty, default specifies a result that will be returned.

max()

The max() method in Python returns as the highest item in the list.

Syntax

maximum (iterable[,key, default])

Here

- A list of objects will be iterable here.
- The key defines a single-argument function for extracting a comparison key from each list member.
- If the iterable is empty, the default specifies a result that will be returned.

sorted()

The Python sorted() function takes an iterable and produces a sorted list of objects.

Syntax

sorted(iterable[,key,reverse])

Here

- A list of objects will be iterable here.
- The key defines a single-argument function for extracting a comparison keyword from each list member.
- The reverse is a book that determines whether the sorting must be done in descending or ascending order (False or True). False is the default value.

reversed()

Python's reversed() method provides a reverse iterator, which we can use to request the next item or iterate until we reach the end.

Syntax

reversed(iterator)

It's worth noting the following:

- We can use list() to produce the list of items since reversed() returns a generator expression.
- The reversed() function in Python is comparable to the reversed() method in the list method (). The latter, on the other hand, inverts the list in place.
- We can reverse a list using slicing(a[:-1]), which is analogous to the reversed() method.

enumerate()

The Python enumerate() method produces an enumerate object from which we may iterate till we reach the end or request the next item.

enumerate(sequence, start=0) enumerate(sequence, start=0) enumerate(sequence, start=

Each subsequent item in the returned object is a tuple (count, item), with the count defaulting to zero and the item obtained by iterating over the iterator.

zip()

Python's zip() method provides an iterator that includes an aggregate of each iterable's item.

Syntax

zip(*iterables)

map()

Produces an iterator after mapping a method to each element of iterable in Python.

[map(function, iterable,]

We use this function when we don't want to use the usual for loop and want to execute a function to each item in iterable.

filter()

The Python filter() function creates an iterator from iterable objects that meet the criteria.

Syntax

filter(function, iterable)

The function parameter specifies the condition that the iterable's elements must meet. Items that do not meet the requirements are eliminated.

iter()

The iter() method in Python turns iterable to an iterator, from which we may request the next element or iterate until we reach the end.

Syntax

iter(object[,sentinel])

Here

- Depending on whether a sentinel is present, an object may be represented differently. It is an iterable or sequence if a sentinel isn't supplied; otherwise, it should be a callable object.
- The sentinel defines a value that will be used to identify the sequence's end.

all()

all() returns True whether all elements of an iterable were true or if the iterable is blank in Python.

Syntax

all(iterable)

- False; empty list([]), strings(''), dict(); zero(0), None, and so on are all false in Python.

- Because the Python all() method accepts an iterable argument, it will return True if an empty list is supplied as an input. It will, however, return False if a list containing empty lists is supplied.

any()

When at least one item in the iterable is true, the Python any() method returns True. If iterable is empty, it will return False, unlike all().

Syntax

any(iterable)

Code

Check if at least one item of the list ['hi',[4,9],-4,True] is true.

l1 = ['hi',[4,9],-4,True] # all is true

any(l1)

True

l2 = ['',[],{},False,0,None] # all is false

any(l2)

False

6.2: Tuples

Many typical characteristics of lists and strings, such as indexing & slicing operations, have been shown. Sequence data types include list, tuple, and range (Sequence Types — list, tuple). Other sequence types of data may well be introduced since Python is a developing language. There's also the tuple, which is a typical sequence data type. A tuple is a compilation/collection of values separated by commas.

To ensure that nested tuples were properly processed, output tuples always are wrapped in parenthesis; they may be entered with or without enclosing parentheses, but parentheses are often required regardless (if the tuple is a larger expression). It is not feasible to assign individual elements in a tuple. However, tuples containing mutable structures, such as lists, may be created.

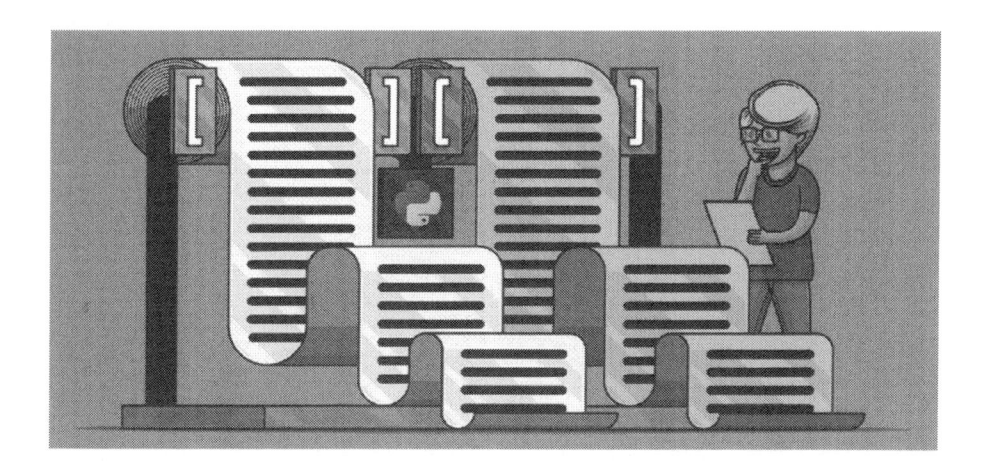

Despite their resemblance to lists, tuples are often utilized in distinct settings and for different reasons. Tuples are immutable and often include a homogeneous sequence of components that may be retrieved by unpacking (discussed further below) or indexing. Lists are changeable, their items are homogenous, and they may be accessed by repeating them.

Forming tuples with 0 or 1 elements is a difficulty, and the syntax has had some additional peculiarities to address this. An empty set of parentheses constructs an empty tuple; a tuple including one item is built by continuing a number with a value with

Why not use a list instead of a tuple?

- Program execution is quicker than manipulating a list when managing a tuple. (When the list and tuple are tiny, this is unlikely to be noticed.)

- There are occasions when you don't want the information to be changed. Using a tuple rather than a list protects against unintentional alteration if the values inside the collection are expected to stay constant for the duration of the application.

- Another Python type of data you'll soon encounter is a dictionary, which needs an immutable type of value among its components. Rather than a list, a tuple can also be used for such a purpose.

A tuple is indeed a collection of ordered and immutable items.

Getting Values in Tuples

To get values from a tuple, use brackets for slicing and the index multiple indices to get the values that are accessible at that index. For instance,

Tuples Updating

Tuple elements are immutable, so you can't update or modify their values. You may generate new tuples by combining parts of existing tuples.

Tuple Elements Deletion

Individual tuple elements cannot be removed. Simply use the

del command to erase a whole tuple.

6.3: Built-in Functions

abs(x)

Returns a number's absolute value. An integer, a precision floating-point number, or an object that implements __abs__ may be used as the parameter (). The magnitude of the input is returned if it is a complex number.

aiter(async iterable)

For each asynchronous iterable, return an asynchronous iterator. It's the same as calling x. aiter__ ().

Unlike iter(), aiter() does not have a two-argument variation.

all(iterable)

Return True if the iterable's components are all true (or if the iterable is empty).

Code

def all(iterable):

   for element in iterable:

      if not, element:

         return False

return True

available next(async iterator[, default]),

Return the next item from the specified asynchronous iterator when awaited, or default if no iterator is given as well as the iterator becomes exhausted.

That's the async version of next() built-in, but it works similarly.

It executes the async iterator's __anext__() function, which returns an available. Awaiting this provides the iterator's next value. The default is returned if the iterator is completed; otherwise, StopAsyncIteration is triggered.

any(iterable)

If any element of iterable is true, return True. Return False if iterable is empty.

ascii(object)

Return a string providing a printable image of an object, but use the x, u, or U escapes to escape any non-ASCII characters within the string provided by repr(). It produces a string that looks like the one provided by repr() Python 2.

(*args, **kws) breakpoint

This function takes you to the call site's debugger. It specifically calls sys.breakpointhook() and passes args and kws to it. sys.breakpointhook() calls pdb.set trace() with no parameters

by default. In this instance, it's only a convenience method, so you don't have to specifically import pdb or write quite so much code to get into the debugger. However, sys.breakpointhook() may be assigned to any other function, and breakpoint() will call it automatically, enabling you to debug with your preferred debugger.

With the input breakpointhook, it fires an auditing event builtins.breakpoint.

bytearray class ([source[, encoding[, errors]]])

Return a new byte array. The byte array subclass is a changeable series of integers ranging from 0 to 256. It has most of the mutable sequence types of methods, as defined in Changeable Sequence Types, and most of the bytes type's methods, as detailed in Bytes & Bytearray Operations.

The array may be initialized in a variety of ways using the optional source parameter:

- If it's a string, you'll additionally need to provide the

encoding (and errors) options; byte array() will then use str.encode to convert the sequence to bytes ().

- If it's an integer, the array will be that size, and null bytes will be used to start it.

- A read-only object buffer will be utilized to populate the bytes array if it is an object that conforms to the buffer interface.

- If it's iterable, it'd be an iterable containing number within the range 0 to 256 that is used as the array's initial contents.

Chapter 7: File Handling

Unless you're working with a large software program that processes a large amount of data, you shouldn't anticipate the data to be kept in a variable since variables have a short lifespan. Consequently, while dealing with such instances, the function of papers will become more important to consider. Our applications will manage files using Python since files are non-volatile, meaning the data would be permanently kept in secondary storage such as a hard drive. Are you thinking about how Python should deal with files at this point? Consider how the general public will manage the files. The standard read/write operations on a file must be performed first (or a new file must be created if the file does not yet exist), and then the file must be saved and closed once the usual read/write operations have been completed.

We can do the same operations in Python similarly by utilizing built-in methods and functions. Why is there this stir and uproar about something so inconsequential? The treatment may be performed as many times as necessary as the data is little; however, if the data is large, it will be unable to conduct recurrent treatment, and the processed data will have to be preserved. Here comes the job of information storage and transfer to a file into the computer system, which is important.

When data is being written into a record, it is critical to remember that the integrity and authenticity of the information must be preserved. Following the saving of your data to the file, the most important step is retrieving it. Data is kept in computers as binary bits of 1s and 0s; if the retrieval procedure is not completed properly, the data becomes completely unusable; this is referred to as corrupted data. To do this, file Handling using Python is a multi-faceted procedure that involves both writing and reading data.

7.1: Editing Files

In Python document code, two types of files may be managed, and each of them is explained in detail with several examples for your convenience. There are two types of files: binary files and text files. Binary files are the most common kind of file. Binary files account for the vast majority of the data we access on our computers. All binary files have a common format that they all follow. Even while we can open some data files with a conventional text editor, we cannot access the information. All binary files are encoded in binary, which a machine can only interpret, and this is indeed the case in this situation. We'll need a particular piece of software to open binary files of this kind. Text files do not need any special encoding and can be opened with about any text editor compatible with text files.

It's very versatile, easy to understand and analyze, and visually attractive to look at. Python is considered one of the best toolboxes for developing features and tools that you'll use for various reasons in the programming world. Python is scalable and has a large number of features. Python has built-in methods for generating and manipulating files, notably flat and text files, and working with data arrays. Because the io module is the industry standard for reading files, we won't have to import other libraries to do routine IO operations. The file management functions open(), stop(), read(), write(), or append() are the most important in Python (). Python has file management capabilities, allowing users to read and write documents and conduct various other file-related tasks via scripts. The concept of memory management has been extended to various additional styles. However, the implementation is either hard or time-consuming to complete.

The open() Function

We use the open () function of the Python programming language to open any file-handling script file in either reading or writing mode. We make use of the open () function in Python. As previously indicated, the function open () returns an object representing a file. To produce a file object, we use the open () method with two arguments: the file name and the

mode, which specifies whether to read English to the file. Consequently, the following syntax is open (filename, mode). When it comes to opening files, Python has three distinct ways to choose from:

- " r " is an abbreviation for " read."
- "w" is an abbreviation for "write."
- Reading and writing are both possible with the letter "r."

Important to know is that the mode option is not necessary in this case. If the value is not specified, Python will presume it is " r " as default. Reading a file may be accomplished in various ways in Python file-handling routines. We may be able to make use of a file. Read a file to extract a string that comprises all of the letters contained inside it (). The whole code might look something like this:

Example Code

py = open("file1.text", "r")

print (py.read())

We must first open the file in question rather than reading from or writing to a file. It has to be shut off when we're done to release the file's contents.

Using the open function to open a file ()

Using the built-in Python method open() with the argument open a file, one will obtain something known as a file object in response. The File object provides methods and attributes that may be used to acquire information about the topics that have been opened in the File window. These methods and properties are further covered in-depth on this page. It may also be used to amend the previously specified file. The open () function is used for both reading and writing purposes. As previously indicated, it recovers an item in the file format that was previously saved. To manage data files, we employ the open () command in addition to two points of disagreement.

Example Code

py = open("file1.txt", "r")

print (py.read(15))

Python's write() and add() Functions

Let's look at creating a file and how the write mode works: Write the following in the Python environment to amend the file. The write function allows the user to create a new file copy. We must first build the file using one of three main mechanisms: try writing w, append an exclusive, or construction x to be able to read into it using Python. We must proceed with care when employing the w mode since it will erase any previous data in the file, assuming any such data exists. It results in the total deletion of all previously saved information. You may write both a text and a sequence of bytes in a file with PHP's write () function, available in most programming languages. This algorithm produces an integer containing the number of characters written to the file due to the operation. There must be no existing file called test.txt in the current working directory for this program to work; otherwise, it will generate a new file named test.txt. If it is present, it will take precedence over any other option. It is necessary to add the newline characters to differentiate between the several lines.

Example Code

pyfile = open('helloworld.txt','w')

pyfile.write("This program is an example code. ")

pyfile.close()

Close () in file management

The file-handling code instruction close () ends all resources now in use and frees up the system from the restrictions imposed by this specific application. Python's close () method is used to close a file that the user has already opened. A file that has been sealed cannot be read or changed in any way. Any operation that requires the file to also be opened will result in a value error if the file has indeed been closed after it has been opened. It is permitted to use close () numerous times in a single program session. Because of this, it is intended to make grammar and error handling clearer while working with programming languages and programs.

As a result, using them in combination with a statement is a good idea when the situation calls for it. As a consequence of using this method, any active folders will be closed as soon as they are finished, resulting in improved performance across the engine. The importance of explicitly removing each open file after its work has been done and there is no longer a need to keep it open cannot be overstated. Given that there is a cap on the number of files that a single piece of software may open at a time if you go over that limitation, there is also no practical method to recover from this situation, and the program may collapse as a consequence of the overload. This technique's close() function is not secure when used. As a result, if the lone exception happens when the code is doing some activity on the file, its function exits without shutting down the file due to the detected error.

Example Code

pyfile = open('helloworld.txt','a')

pyfile.write("This will add data to a specific line.")

pyfile.close()

Python is a programming language that is one of the most sophisticated and commonly utilized currently accessible. This programming language is straightforward to develop and analyze, making it excellent for beginning programmers.

Furthermore, it is a good location for young programmers to begin their careers because of its versatility. Python offers straightforward functions with quick response times and robust error management techniques, making the creation and debugging processes significantly less unpleasant than other programming languages.

7.2: Directory Contents

We may need to get a list of all files included inside a specific directory when collaborating with Python.

Using os module

The os module of Python has a method that returns a listing of files included inside a directory. The letter. supplied as an input to the functioning OS. listdir(), denotes the current directory.

To get a list of files located at a certain path, we may provide the path to the function as a string.

Alternatively, if you're not dealing with documents, the path must be local to where the Python file is. If you're not working using files, the path must be local to where the Python Shell has indeed been launched:

Example Code

os.listdir('file1/Music')

Making use of the glob module

It is also feasible to list files included inside a directory using the glob module.

Using the glob technique, we can also recursively output the filenames. A recursive argument must be specified in the method call.

Example Code

for filename in glob.iglob('file1/**/*.txt', recursive=True):

　print(filename)

The code above will repeatedly look for all .txt files in the Desktop folder and print them. We can substitute *.txt with a single * to output all files in a folder.

Using the ** command, you may search for items recursively. This command is only relevant when the recurrent parameter is set to True.

Chapter 8: Exception Handling In Python

An exception is defined as a condition in a program that is out of the ordinary and causes the program's flow to be interrupted. Whenever the exception occurs, the program terminates the current execution and prevents the subsequent code from being performed. As a result, the only exception is when a Python script encounters run-time issues that it cannot manage. When something goes wrong, another is a Python object the problem. Python provides a mechanism for dealing with exceptions, allowing the code to continue to run without being interrupted. It is possible that if we do not manage an exception, the interpreter will not execute all of the code that follows the exception.

What Are The Different Types Of Python Exceptions?

A variety of causes, including those listed above, can result in exceptions in Python programs. If these exceptions aren't managed properly, they might cause the program to crash, resulting in data loss or, in the worst-case scenario, corrupted data. As a Python developer, you must anticipate and incorporate error handling into your code to avoid potential problems. On the other hand, Python is equipped with a comprehensive error handling mechanism. Python applications may determine their error type at run time by employing structured exception processing and a set of pre-defined exceptions. It allows them to respond appropriately. These can involve taking a different route, using default settings, or prompting the user for the necessary information.

Frequently Occurring Exceptions

Python has many built-in exceptions; however, we will cover this section's most frequent standard exceptions.

1. One type of error is the ZeroDivisionError, which occurs when a value is divided by 0.

2. NameError: This error happens when a given name cannot be found. It could be external or internal in scope.

3. IndentationError: If the indentation is incorrectly specified.

4. It occurs when an operation involving Input-Output fails (IOError).

5. EOFError: This error occurs when the end of a file is reached while actions are still being done.

8.1: Try And Except

When an exception occurs in Python, the try and except commands are used to capture and deal with it.

Example Code

a = [1, 2, 3]

try:

    print ("Second element = %d" %(a[1]))

    print ("Fourth element = %d" %(a[3]))

except:

    print ("An error occurred")

In the above sample, the statements that have the potential to produce an error are contained within the try function. It occurs because the new print statement attempts to access the fifth element of the list, which is not present, and as a result, an exception is raised unless a statement is responsible for catching this exception.

8.2: Exception Handling For A Specific Exception

If a try statement has more least one except clause, the handlers for the different exceptions can be specified for each clause. Keep in mind that only one handler would be executed at a time. For example, we could include the IndexError exception in the code above. The following is the standard syntax for adding special exceptions: –

8.3: Try And Else Clause In Exception Handling

When using the try-except block in Python, you may utilize the else clause. This clause must be included in the except clauses. After entering the else block, the code checks to see if the attempt clause has not raised an exception.

Example Code

def AbyB(a , b):

    try:

        c = ((a+b) / (a-b))

    except ZeroDivisionError:

        print ("a/b result in 0")

    else:

        print (c)

AbyB(2.0, 3.0)

AbyB(3.0, 3.0)

8.4: Keyword In Exception Handling

After the if and except blocks, Python provides the term finally, which is always performed after them. The final block is always executed after the try block has completed its usual operation or after the try block has completed its operation owing to an exception.

Code:

try:

    k = 5//0 # raises divide by zero exception.

    print(k)

except ZeroDivisionError:

    print("Can't divide by zero")

finally:

    print('executed')

8.5: Raising Exception

The raise statement enables a programmer to cause the occurrence of a certain exception to take place. Raise takes only one argument, which specifies the exception to raise. It is either an instance of an exception or a class of exceptions.

Code:

try:

    raise NameError("EXCEPTION HANDLING") # Raise Error

except NameError:

    print ("This is an exception")

8.6: Advantages of Exception Handling

Bugs & errors are a normal part of the development process for any developer. As previously stated, the distinction between mistakes and exceptions is important. Consequently, why is it important for Python developers to understand how to manage Python errors and catch Python exceptions? Instead, let's look at a real-world application. For example, suppose you're dealing with a large volume of data. As a result, you create software that can read thousands of files from numerous folders. There is no chance of avoiding encountering an error in this situation. Among the possible mistakes is the use of the incorrect or absent file type, the use of an invalid file format, and the use of multiple file extensions. As a result, it is not viable to open all of the files and develop a script that can cater to their needs quickly. Exception handling allows developers to define many conditions in a single code block. For example, you can resolve any invalid format by first making an accurate format and then reading the file after that has been established. It is also possible to proceed with reading the data while skipping over the files that have an incorrect format. Then, establish a log that will be used to deal with that later in the process. APMs like Retrace are excellent tools for dealing with log files and can assist you in your efforts. It provides logging capabilities and actionable information to assist you in developing Python applications.

Chapter 9: Data Science and Python

Before we go into how to study Python with data science, it's important to first understand why you can learn Python in the first place. In conclusion, knowing Python was among the most important skills for a data science profession.

Python is the programming preferred language for data science, albeit it hasn't always been. Here's a quick rundown of the past:

- It surpassed R in Kaggle, the leading platform in data science contests, in 2016.

- It surpassed R in KDNuggets' annual survey of data scientists' most utilized tools in 2017.

- In 2018, 66% of all data analysts said they used Python daily, making it the most popular language among analytics experts.

Experts in data scientists believe that this tendency will continue as the Python environment develops. While your quest to understand Python programming could be just getting started, it's comforting to know that job prospects are plenty (and rising).

According to Indeed, the average income for the Data Scientist is $121,583.

So, data science has a bright future, and Python is only one puzzle component. Fortunately, learning Python and other programming essentials is as simple as possible. In five easy steps, we'll show you how.

But keep in mind that because the processes are straightforward doesn't mean you won't have to work hard. You could not only acquire a new talent but also take your career to a different level if you apply yourselves and devote serious time to studying Python.

Is Python Essential in the Field of Data Science?

Working as a data scientist may be done with either Python or otherwise R. Both languages have advantages and disadvantages, and they are extensively used in the business. R is more common in specific sectors, although Python is more popular overall. You'll certainly need to master at least a few of these second languages to work in data science. It is not Python, but it must be one of the two options: Python or R. (Of course, regardless of whether you choose Python or R as your main programming language, you'll need to learn SQL.)

Is Python a Better Data Science Tool Than R?

It is a frequently debated issue in data science; however, the real answer would be that it varies on what you're searching for and what people like.

R was created with mathematics and statistics in mind, and several fantastic tools make data science a breeze. It also has a sizeable/large online community that is highly supportive. Python is a far superior language for general-purpose tasks; thus, your Python abilities will be more transferable to other fields. It's also significantly more popular, and several say it's the simpler to learn of the two. Rather than reading views, look at this more impartial comparison of how Python & R handle comparable data science jobs and determine which one appeals to you.

What is Python's Role in Data Science?

Python and other programming languages are employed at every stage of the data science procedure. A data science experiment pipeline, for example, may look like this:

1. You build a query in Python and SQL to get the data they need through your company's database.

2. You clean & organize the data into a table data frame ready for analysis using Python and the panda's module.

3. You begin analyzing, investigating, and visualizing the data using Python or the pandas & matplotlib tools.

4. After understanding more about data via your investigation, you use Python and the scikit-learn module to create a prediction model based on the information you gathered.

5. You structure your final analysis plus model findings suitable for sharing with your teammates.

Python is utilized at every stage of the process!

9.1: Jupyter Notebook

Jupyter Notebook would be a free and open-source online tool that allows you to work with data interactively. It generates papers (notebooks) with both inputs (code) & outputs in one file. It provides a single page with • Visualizations

- Equations in mathematics
- Statistical analysis
- Some other rich media
- Narrative text

Users may build, display the findings, and add information, graphs, & formulae to make work more understandable, repeatable, and shared using this one document method.

Jupyter notebooks support over forty programming computer

languages, with Python being the most popular.

Anyone may use it for data science since it is an open and free tool. The Jupyter notebook comes in two flavors

- Jupyter Classic Notebook, which includes all the features.
- JupyterLab, the new next-generation notebooks interface that's more expandable and modular, supports a broad range of data science, machine learning, & scientific computing activities.

JupyterLab is now the standard notebook for all Jupyter projects.

Jupyter Notebook, which sprang from IPython in 2014, has been widely adopted by the field of data analytics to the point that it has become the preferred setting for study. Because this handy tool allows multi-language programming, it has become the de-facto option for data scientists when it comes to practicing and sharing multiple codes, rapid prototyping, and exploratory analysis.

Although there are several language-specific IDEs such as PyCharm, Spyder, or Atom, Jupyter has risen in popularity among data scientists due to its flexibility and instructiveness. Jupyter Notebook has also garnered popularity as an educational tool in the digital humanities. According to GitHub research, more than 2.5 million accessible Jupyter notebooks were shared during September 2018, increasing the 200,000 recorded in 2015. So, before we go into the capabilities and benefits of Jupyter and why it is regarded as the greatest environment for data scientists, let's first define a Jupyter Notebook.

What Is Jupyter Notebook, and How Do I Use It?

Julia, Python, and R are three languages that have been combined in an indirect acronym. Jupyter Notebook is an online tool that enables users to write and exchange programs, equations, visualizations, and text. The notebook is a multi-language collaborative computing environment that supports more than forty programming languages. Users may use Jupyter Notebook to combine data, code, and text to create an engaging computational tale.

Jupyter Notebook may mix scripts and instructions/explanations with the application's interactivity to analyze a corpus of written content, create music or art, or build engineering ideas. As a result, data scientists may use it to streamline end-to-end data science procedures. Python pip command may be used to install the Jupyter Notebook. And, if you're using Anaconda, it'll be installed as part of an Anaconda installation. The notebook applications, kernels, & notebook papers are the three components that make it up. Notebook web applications can be used for interactively creating and executing programs, but kernels govern the system by running & introspecting users' codes. Finally, notebook papers are self-contained documents that include all the material seen in the notebook. The kernel manages each page in the notebook.

Jupyter has become the de-facto standard for data scientists, according to Lorena Barba, a mechanical & aeronautical engineer from Washington George University in DC.

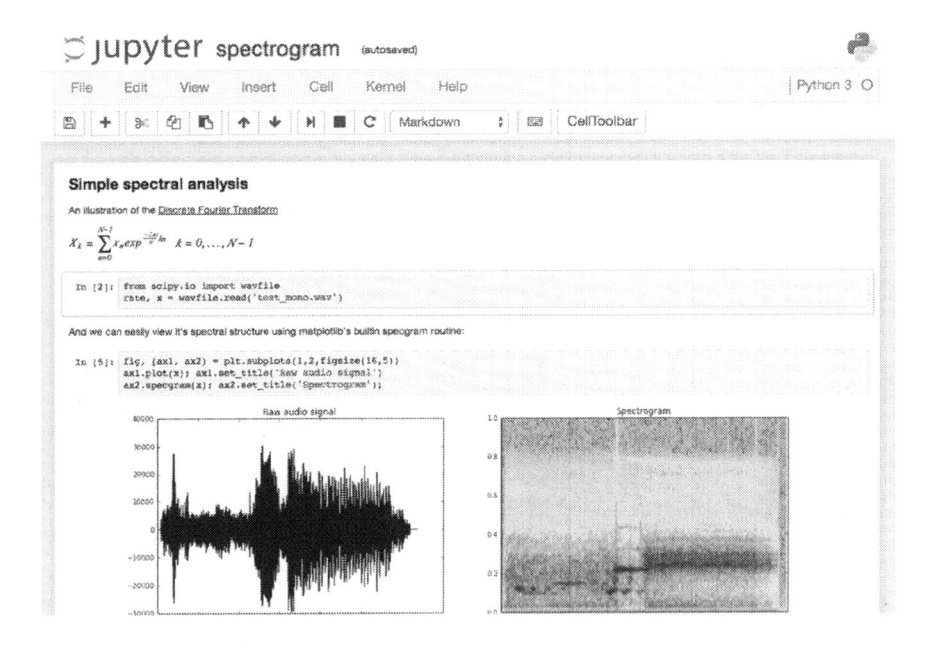

Jupyter Notebook's Purpose

- Cleaning of data
- Statistical Analysis
- ML Model Training
- Visualization of data

What makes Notebook Jupyter So Special? De facto Selection

Jupyter Notebook has grown common among data scientists due to the expanding popularity of mainstream applications in

the business and the fast expansion of machine learning and data science. This interactive web-based cloud computing environment allows multi-language programming and provides Markdown cells, enabling more extensive write-ups with simple formatting. The finished output may be produced as a PDF and HTML file that can be viewed in a browser or shared on places like GitHub using Jupyter. Jupyter Notebooks are stored as JSON structured text files, making them exceedingly simple to distribute.

Jupyter's success, according to Fernando Pérez, cofounder, is attributable to advancements in the web software that runs apps like Gmail and Google Docs, as well as the simplicity with which it permits access to distant data that would otherwise be hard to download. Another explanation for this platform's success is the maturity of scientific Python & data science.

Jupyter Notebooks have also been critical in the industrialization of computer science, allowing access by lowering entrance hurdles for data scientists.

Benefits

Although Jupyter was originally designed for data applied

sciences written in languages such as Python, R, and Julia, it is currently utilized for many tasks. Besides that, Jupyter makes documentation and visualizations, especially caching, a lot simpler, particularly for non-technical people, by reducing the hurdles for data scientists.

"Jupyter Notebook must be an intrinsic component of every Python data scientist's toolset," a data science enthusiast remarked. It's ideal for developing and sharing visualization notes."

Jupyter enables users to observe the results of their code in real-time without waiting for other sections of the code to finish. Every cell of a code in the notebook may be examined to generate an output at any moment. As a result, unlike other typical IDEs such as PyCharm and VSCode, Jupyter allows for in-line printing of results, which is particularly beneficial for data analysis (EDA).

- Easy Caching with Built-In Cell: It's tough to keep track of each cell's processing status, but Jupyter takes overhaul/care of it for you, whether it's a code that's training a Machine learning model or even a code that's downloading terabytes of data from a distant server, Jupyter stores the results of each cell that's executing.

- Jupyter Notebook is both platforms- and language-independent due to its encoding in JSON format. Another advantage is that Jupyter may be processed in various languages and converted to file formats, including Markdown, HTML, and PDF.

- Data Visualization: Shared notebook Jupyter enables visualizations as a component, which involves visualizing certain data sets, such as visuals and charts, created from programs using modules such as Plotly, Matplotlib, or Bokeh. Jupyter allows users to narrate visualizations and share code and data sets, allowing others to make changes interactively.

- Live Code Interactions: The Jupyter Notebook uses the "ipywidgets" packages, which provide user interfaces for interacting with code and data. It enables users to manage code input sources and offer feedback directly via the browser.

- Documenting Samples Code: Jupyter makes it simple for users to describe their code line by line, with feedback attached. Even better, Jupyter allows users to add interactivity and explanations to their code while keeping it completely functional.

9.2: Data Dealing

Python programming offers a wide range of frameworks and functionality for graphical user interfaces, online application development, data processing, & data visualization, among other things. Although the Python programming language is not perfect for web applications, it is widely utilized by many businesses for assessing massive datasets, data visualization, data analysis, and prototyping. The Python programming computer language is gaining popularity among data scientists despite being obsolete as a web computer language. This chapter aims to compare the two very distinct reasons for using Python and demonstrate that knowing Python as a web computer language is not required for undertaking machine learning in Python.

Python as a Data Science Tool

The Python programming language is used by businesses of all sizes and sectors, from the largest investment banks to the tiniest big data startups. Python data sciences programming language is among big data corporations and digital startups. It is one of the top ten computer languages to learn in 2015.

"There are only two sorts of languages: those about which people complain and those which no one uses." Bjarne

Stroustrup, Bjarne Stroustrup, Bjarne Stroustrup, Bjar.

The Python programming language falls under the first group, and it is gaining popularity in numerical calculations, machine learning, and a variety of data science applications. Except for performance-critical and low-level tasks, the Python language can accomplish everything. For data and research calculations, Python is the finest programming language to employ. Learning Python programming for website designing necessitates programmers' proficiency in various web frameworks, such as Django, that aid in creating websites, whereas having to learn Python for data scientists necessitates data scientists' proficiency in regular expressions, scientific libraries, and data visualizations concepts. With various uses, programmers or experts who are not familiar with web programming ideas or the Python programming language may easily study data science in the Python programming language.

Python is a 23-year-old strong expressive, dynamic programming language that allows a programmer to write code once and execute it without needing a separate compiler. Python supports a variety of programming paradigms in web development, including structured programming, functional programming, and object-oriented programming. Python code may easily be integrated into various current web applications that need a programming interface. On the other hand, Python is the language of choice for academic, research, and scientific applications that need quick execution and exact mathematical computations.

Python web programming necessitates knowledge of the numerous python website development frameworks, which may be scary due to the python website development framework documentation being difficult to comprehend. However, knowing a web framework is unavoidable if you want to create a dynamic website or online application using Python.

9.3: DataFrames

If you're a Python developer or programmer, you've heard of Pandas, one of the best Python packages. Pandas have evolved into a common data analysis tool and management in Python over the years. Other useful Python utilities may be found here. Pandas is undoubtedly the most flexible Python data science tool for a good reason. Data Frames in Python are one of the strong, expressive, & flexible data structures it offers for simple data manipulation and analysis.

What is Data Frame, and how does it work?

A Data Frame is a "two-dimensional, size-mutable, possibly heterogeneous tabular data model with named axes (rows and columns)," according to the Pandas library documentation. In basic terms, the Data Frame is a data structure in which data is organized in columns and rows in a tabular format.

The following are common qualities of a Data Frame:

- It might contain a lot of rows and columns.
- Each column has a separate variable that characterizes the samples, shaped by several data sets (rows).
- All the data in each column is of the same kind
- It prevents missing values so that there are no spaces or empty value systems between rows or columns, unlike excel data sets.

You may also define the index & column titles for the Data Frame inside a Pandas Data Frame. The column names reveal the difference in columns, whereas the index shows the difference in rows.

In Python, this is how to make a data frame (Using Pandas)

The first step in Python data munging is to create a Data Frame. You may create a Pandas Frame using the following inputs:

- Lists
- Dict
- Series

- "ndarray" in Numpy
- CS files (external files)
- Additional data frame

What Are The Most Basic Data-Frame Operations?

It's time to learn about various operations inside a Data Frame now that we've seen three distinct methods to build Data Frames in Python.

1. Choosing a column or index from the Pandas Data Frame

Before you can start adding, removing, and renaming any components inside a DataFrame, you must first understand how to choose an index or column. Assume the following is the Data Frame.

```
   A B C
0  1 2 3
1  4 5 6
2  7 8 9
```

You're looking for index zero under column 'A,' 1. There are many methods to get at this number, but the most essential is .loc[] and .iloc[].

```
script.py   IPython Shell
1   # Using `iloc[]`
2   print(df.iloc[0][0])
3
4   # Using `loc[]`
5   print(df.loc[0]['A'])
6
7   # Using `at[]`
8   print(df.at[0,'A'])
9
10  # Using `iat[]`
11  print(df.iat[0,0])
```

Run

```
script.py   IPython Shell
1
1
1
<script.py> output:
1
1
1
1
In [1]:
```
Great work!

Run

2. Creating a new column

If you wish to incorporate/include an index in a Data Frame, one may assign a column from Data Frame or a reference to a column that hasn't been generated yet to such as this .index property.

3. How to Remove a Pandas DataFrame Row, Index, or Column

Getting rid of an index

- Resetting the Data Frame's index.

- Using del df.index. Name function, remove this same index name (if any).

- Remove an index and a row together.

- Reset the index, remove the duplicates of an index column that has been introduced to a Data Frame, and reinstate the new column as the index.

Removing a column from the table

The drop() method may remove columns from the Data Frame.

Why are Pandas among the most popular Python packages for creating data frames?

The Pandas library is thought to be the finest for building data frames since it has several characteristics that make it easy to do so. The following are some of these characteristics: Pandas provide various data frames that allow us to represent data efficiently and change it. It has effective alignment and indexing characteristics that allow for intelligent data labeling and organization. Pandas have certain characteristics that make the code cleaner and easier to understand, creating a more efficient. It can read a variety of file types. Pandas support a variety of file formats, including CSV, JSON, HDF5, and Excel. Combining numerous datasets has proven to be a difficult task for many programmers. Pandas can also overcome this and combine numerous data sets highly effectively.

Chapter 10: Python and Game Development

Any previous beliefs about game development and coding, in general, should be thrown out the window. Most of what you see in films and television is based on computer technology, whether it's the script and numerous characters who fill a computer display or the concentrated staring and tinkering of the individual in front of every computer monitor.

Nonetheless, my point would be that learning to develop a game is not a mindless activity. Coding also has a terrific time, ingenuity, and magnificence that flows into (and out of) it and a fantastic time.

Because a scripting language is nothing but a way of conveying instructions to an electronic device, once the code has been copied, the result is magnificent, powerful, and, most importantly, precious.

One of the most effective ways to expose your child to coding is via video games. A programming language, including JavaScript, may bring your child's wild world and interesting character notions to life using a programming language such as JavaScript. Every game is built based on code. The coding of a game is what provides it its life. It is the driving force behind the movement of characters and adversaries' attacks.

It is possible to create the foundation of a game by employing models and gameplay elements, but there is no movement, interactivity, or game management available without using computer code.

A computer game, often known as a video game, is an electronic game that utilizes an interface or computers mouse to provide visual cues, such as a gamepad, joystick, keyboard, or movement detecting device, to engage the player's attention. This feedback is shown visually on a visual display device such as a television, monitor, tablet, or VR technology headset. In video games, audio feedback is provided by speakers or headphones, and other types of feedback, including haptic technology, are also often employed to enhance the gaming experience.

Video games are divided into arcade games, console games, and personal computer (PC) games. Video games are classified into a range of genres based on the kind of gameplay and the purpose they are intended to achieve.

When video games were first developed in the 1950s early 1960s, they were simple adaptations of existing electronic games that made use of video-like output from large room-sized computers, a technology that is still in use today. The video arcade game was the earliest commercial video game released in 1971. In 1972, Pong, the iconic arcade game, and the Magnavox Odyssey, the world's first personal console, made their appearances. The North American computer industry crisis, which occurred in 1983 due to a loss of publication control and market saturation, had a devastating impact on the quickly expanding sector.

The video game industry emerged due to the crisis, spearheaded by Japanese companies such as Mario, Sega, and the PlayStation, which set standards for creating and marketing computer games, most of which are still in use today. Designers, publishers, marketers, merchants, platforms, as well as other third-party producers, among others, are expected to possess a wide range of competencies.

10.1: Game Development Process

A computer game is a piece of code that contains visuals, audio, and gameplay; as a result, game production is similar to the software development process. When it comes to formal software development methodologies, it is easy to overlook their significance. Poor development processes are more likely to trigger budget and schedule overruns and other issues. Planning may be beneficial for both individual and

Choosing the type of game your young coder wants to create is the most difficult part of game development! Is this a game for the console? Is there a mobile application available? Is there a web-based application available? And, if that's so, in what language(s) is it written?

You should remember that someone learning to become a builder does not start by creating a complete house. Instead, students may choose to construct a chair or practice with specific tools or cuts before moving on to the next step.

Kids will need to start with both the fundamentals, but with repetition and perseverance; they will be able to code anything game their imaginations can conjure up!

C++ and the Development of Video Games

C++ is a sophisticated programming language that allows individuals who master it to solve complex problems and understand how programs operate on a computer.

Visual Studio, also known as an IDE, is a program that young people can use to construct C++ applications. It is a platform utilized by the entire gaming industry, and it includes a variety of features and services to assist.

Children may use their C++ programming skills to create something like an RPG battle tournament, in which they may create, save, and reload characters, track character triumphs and stats, and code spin battling in a loop to select the winner.

You can create parameters and classes and entities and arrays and procedures and header files, among other things. You can then use visuals to create animation, photos, and movement.

Coding using Drag and Drop

While a traditional technique might have your child designing games utilizing text-based programs, drag-and-drop coding allows your child to create code blocks that visually perform the required action.

GameMaker is a powerful game engine that allows children to create various video games, including role-playing games, 2D platformers, or even point-and-click adventures. Because of its drag-and-drop coding technique, it simplifies the process of creating games, as previously mentioned.

On the other side, children's Scratch coding is a popular option because it can be used to design and develop video games for them. Block-coding may be used to bring computer games back to life with motion and storyline once more, according to the creators. Developers, for example, can simply take and integrate various components of movement or music into their software applications.

Process of Creating a Video Game

What does the process look like for game development since you know what options are accessible in computer languages? So, what is the reason for this action being required?

For a game to be created, it must first be envisioned, with the storyline and plot being developed and other elements like levels and locales, character interactions, etc.

As expected, there are the many other ins and outs to be dealt with and various possibilities available to anyone interested in creating a working and pleasant game.

It is mentioned to set expectations and offer creators a general idea of how to approach the game-building process in general.

Plan

It is possible that planning a project will assist you in staying on track as the job continues. It is also possible to employ a well-thought-out strategy as a roadmap to ensure that the game maker stays true to their original goal.

Video game production necessitates a large commitment of time, cash, and effort on the developer's part. Waste can be decreased if good planning is undertaken.

Game designers may discover that a project element isn't

exactly accurate if proper planning has not been done. The program may have to be re-started or discontinued entirely if the issue is serious enough, depending on the circumstances

10.3: Python Frameworks

Several well-known video games, most notably Battlefield 2, extensively use Python programming for various functions and add-ons. As the gaming industry has advanced, Python has proven to be an excellent choice among developers for rapid prototyping of computer games, particularly in the case of multiplayer games.

1. Pygame

Developed in Python, Pygame is a user-friendly framework that uses the excellent SDL library to construct multimedia such as games. This module uses the programming languages C, Python, and OpenGL. Pygame enables users to develop complete matches and multimedia packages by utilizing Python. It's very portable, and it'll run on any platform and any operating system software without modification.

Some of the qualities include the following:

- Multicore Processors are simple to use and maintain.
- The economical C and Assembly code are employed for

the most fundamental functions.

- It is lightweight and simple to operate.

2. Pyglet

Pyglet is a Language windowing and multimedia program that is open-sourced and works on various operating systems and platforms. For Windows, Os X, and Linux, it's a powerful Python toolkit for designing games and other aesthetically appealing programs that run smoothly. Pyglet supports various features, including windowing, UI event planning, joysticks, OpenGL graphics, loading photographs and videos, and streaming audio and music. In addition to supporting Python 3.5 and higher, Pyglet is also compatible with other Python processors, such as PyPy.

3. PyKyra

Kyra is based on SDL and the Kyra engine, and it is written in Python. The main capabilities of the framework also include support for MPEG movies, sound formats such as MP3 and others, and direct picture reading.

4. Kivy

Kivy is an easily accessible yet cross-platform Python toolkit for rapid application creation that supports new interfaces such as multi-touch apps and existing ones. On Linux, Microsoft Android, iOS, and even Raspberry Pi, Kivy natively supports

most input devices and interfaces. The library is GP-accelerated and includes more gadgets, which are quite extendable in functionality.

5. Panda3d

It is an open-source and unrestricted steam engine written in Python and C++ that can be used to create real-time video games, visual representations, computer models, experiments, and other applications. Several command-line utilities for analyzing and optimizing source materials are included with Panda3D, allowing people to control and script the content generation process. Numerous well-known third-party books are supported, such as the Assimp model loader and the FMOD sound libraries.

6. Python-Ogre

Python-Ogre is a Scripting language interface to the C++ library used by the OGRE 3D engine. A high level of freedom and agility is provided by PyOgre, which is a programming language. It is a 3D modeling engine developed entirely in C++ and used to create several outstanding games. It is composed of two different libraries, which are linked together. Both are

3D rendering engines, with the first being Ogre3d and the other being CEGUi, an integrated user interface system.

10.4: Pygame Python

To put it differently, Python is the most widely used programming language, or to put that another way; Python is the second most widely used programming language. Python is actively involved in developing every emerging field of computer science. Python is home to a large collection of libraries for computer vision (Numpy, Pandas, Matplotlib), intelligent machines (TensorFlow), and a game-development environment (PyGame) (Pygame, Pyglet).

A collection of Extensions for the development of video games, Pygame appears to be an inter accumulation of Extensions for the development of video games.

- It is a set of computer visuals and sound library resources for the Python programming language.
- Pete Shiners created Pygame to fill the void left by PySDL.
- Developing client-side applications that can be packaged as a single-player executable is a strong suit for Pygame.

10.5: Pygame vs. Arcade Coding

Nowadays, game development can be extremely rewarding, and it can also be used for marketing purposes or as a training tool for employees. Game formation involves various skills, including arithmetic, reasoning, physics, machine intelligence, and many others, and it can be extremely enjoyable. Until recently, the Pygame library has been used to accomplish the same task in Python; however, after numerous improvements and dealing with Pygame's problems, a new program, Arcade Library, was created and released. In the following section, we'll discuss how they differ. But first, let us just define what it is they are.

Pygame

It is a Python module that enables you to create elevated and user-interactive computer games by allowing you to use digital animation and sound libraries, among other things. Pygame was created by Pete Shinners, who is also its creator. After that, it was printed underneath the Public License for free software shareware. It was originally developed as a communal effort until 2000. Pygame is portable in that it contains code that is compatible with all operating systems. Also possible is developing open-source, shareware, high price, and commercial games using this framework. Pygame's program is written in C, and the subsystem includes installers for both Windows and Mac OS X systems. Mobile devices, in particular, find it easy to use. Several features were missing from the modules that needed to be added, as explained later in the section's flow.

Arcade

It's another Python module, in this case. However, it is only compatible with Python versions 3.6 and higher. It aspires to provide most of the capabilities which Pygame does not include by default. The use of digital animation and audio resources is also made to develop high and user-interactive games in this manner. Arcade was created by Paul Vincent Craven, who also served as its director. Support for OpenGL 3.3 or higher is required for Arcade. It is compatible with Windows, Linux, and macOS X, built on the OpenGL and Pyglet graphics libraries. Also possible is developing open-source, shareware, premium, and professional games using this framework. It is also compatible with the traditional coordinate system and is extremely simple to use and program.

Chapter 11: GUI in Python

There are no shortage of Python's graphical user interface (GUI) frameworks. Tkinter, WxPython, and Kivy are just a few more popular Python development packages. In addition, there is a slew of what a let GUI packages that "wrap" one of the major packages, such as EasyGUI, PyGUI, and Pyforms, which are all available for download difficulty is that novices (those with less than 6 . months of experience) are unable to learn even the most basic of the major software products, let alone master them. That remains the wrapper package as a possible alternative, but it'll still be virtually impossible for most fresh users to create a custom graphical user interface layout. Even if it is doable, the wrappers will still require several code pages to implement. Python includes a large number of graphical user interface frameworks. However, Tkinter is the only one included in the Python source file. Tkinter has several advantages. Because it is cross-platform, the same code can be used on Windows, macOS, or Linux systems. Applications developed with Tkinter appear to be native to the platform they are run because visual elements are produced utilizing native operating system elements. Even though Tkinter is widely regarded as the legally recognized Python GUI platform, it is not without its detractors.

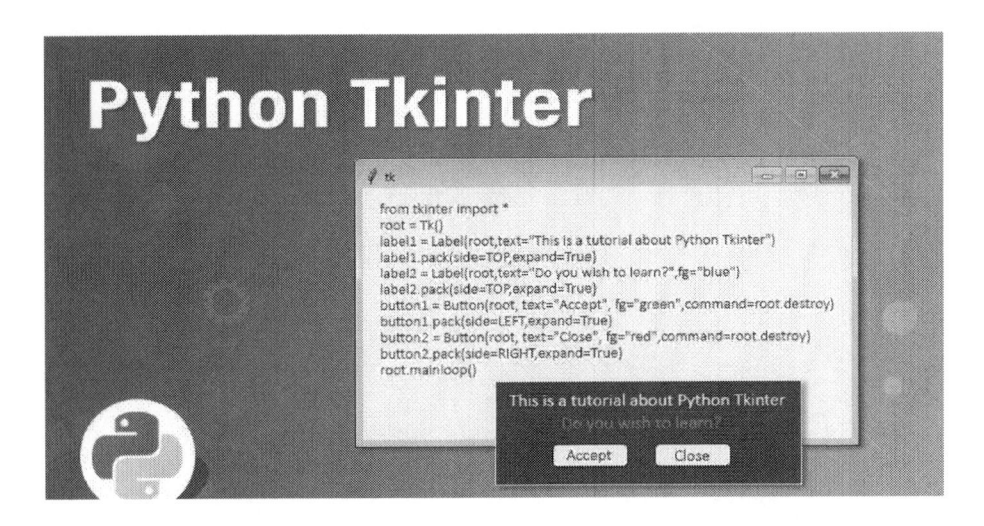

One common complaint is that GUIs created with Tkinter appear to be outdated. If you're hoping for a gleaming, modern interface, Tkinter may not be the best choice for your needs. Comparatively speaking, Tkinter is a lightweight and easy-to-use framework compared to those other frameworks. For Python GUI application development, this makes it an extremely tempting option. It is especially true in situations where current polish is excessive, and the prime aim is to quickly create something functional and cross-platform.

11.1: Building Your First GUI With Tkinter

The window is the most important piece to understand regarding Tkinter GUIs. Windows are now the container whereby all other graphical user interface elements are contained. Widgets are the other graphical user interface elements, such as text boxes, labeling, and buttons used in a program. Widgets are little programs that run inside windows. Create a window that contains only a single widget to begin with. Begin Python shell connection afresh and follow along with the instructions! Once your Python shell is open, the first item you need to do is install a Python GUI Tkinter component from the Python distribution. A window is a Tkinter's Tk class object, which displays information. Proceed to invent a fresh window, then assign this to the property window that was previously defined. An entirely new window appears on your computer screen when you run the code above. Your OS determines its appearance.

(a) Windows (b) macOS (c) Ubuntu

Adding a Widget

Now that you've created a window, you may proceed to add a widget. The tk.Label class can be used to display some text in a window. To begin, create a Label widget with the message "Hello, Tkinter" and set it to a variable named greeting. The window that you previously created remains unchanged. You've just finished creating a Labels widget, but you've not yet included it in the window. There are a variety of approaches to adding widgets to the window. For the time being, you can use the Label widgets.pack() method: The following is how the window now appears. When you cram a widget into a screen, Tkinter shrinks the window to the smallest possible size while still allowing the widget to be seen completely. Now go ahead and do the following. Nothing is happening; however, keep in mind that there is no new prompt in the shell. Python's window.mainloop() instructs it to execute the Tkinter iterator. Once this method has been invoked, it will listen for events such as push buttons or keypresses and prevent any code that follows after it from executing until the window where the method was invoked is closed. You'll notice a new prompt shown in the shell, allowing you to exit your opened window. Creating a window using Tkinter is simple and requires a few lines of code. Blank windows, on the other hand, are not particularly useful! In the following part, you'll learn about some of the widgets available in Tkinter and how to alter them to match the specific demands of your application.

Displaying Text and Images

When you use a label widget, you can show text or images on the screen. The text presented by a Label widget is not editable by the user, and it cannot be changed. It is solely for the sake of presentation. As you saw in the previous example, you can make a Label widget by initializing the Label object and supplying a string to a text parameter: As you saw in the previous example, you can build a Label widget by initializing the Label object and giving a string towards the text parameter. In label widgets, the text is displayed in the system default text color and system default text background color, with the text color being the same as the system text background color. These are normally black and white, but if you've adjusted the color settings on your operating system, you may see a variety of other hues. Because of this, it may appear unusual that although the width and length are set to 10, the label displayed in the window is not square. Because width and length are defined in text units, this is the case. In the standard system font, the letter zero, or the numeral zero, is used to determine the width of one horizontal text unit. In the same way, the height of character zero determines the length of one vertical text unit.

Example Code

```
label = tk.Label(
    text="Hello, Tkinter",
    foreground="white"
    background="black"
)
```

Displaying Clickable Buttons

Button widgets are also used to display buttons that can be clicked on. You can customize them to do a certain purpose whenever they are clicked. In the following part, you'll learn how to invoke functions from the actions of clicking buttons. For the time being, let's look at where to design and decorate a button. When it comes to widgets, the Button or Label widgets have a lot in common. When it comes down to it, a button is simply a label that you can click! It is possible to build and style Button widgets using the same keyword parameters that you are using to create and design Label widgets. A button with a background color and yellow text, for example, is created with the following code.

Example Code

```
button = tk.Button(
    text="Click me!",
    width=25,
    height=5,
    bg="blue",
    fg="yellow",
)
```

Getting User Input

You can use an Entry widget when you need to collect a little amount of text from such a user, such as a user's name/email address. It will display a little text box into which the user can enter some text if they so choose. Creating and customizing an Entry widget is similar to creating and styling Label and Buttons widgets. A widget with such a blue field, some yellow textual, and size of fifty text units can be created with the following code; for example, entry equals to tk.

It is the method of obtaining feedback from an important user. Entry widgets can be used to execute three major operations: input, validation, and validation.

1. Retrieving text using the.get() function
2. Deleting text using the.delete() function ()
3. Using the.insert command to insert text ()

The most effective way to gain knowledge of Entry widgets is to construct one and interact with it directly. To follow the exercises in this section, open a Python terminal and type "python." To begin, import Tkinter and start a new window in your browser. The label specifies the type of text that should be entered into the Entry widget. It does not impose any requirements just on entry, but it does inform the user of what your program wants them to provide in the entry. It is necessary to .pack() the widgets into the window to be visible.

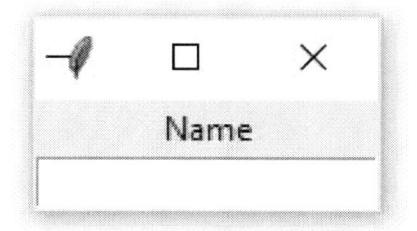

Now that you've put some text into the Entry widget, it hasn't been transferred to your program yet, but it will be soon. You can retrieve the text by calling the function get() and assigning it to a named variable. Text can also be removed from a document. Python's.delete() method accepts an integer parameter that specifies which character should be removed from the string. For instance, the code below demonstrates how the function. Delete (0) removes the initial character from the string Entry. Entry.delete() behaves in the same way as string slicing.

The first parameter determines the starting index, and the deletion proceeds up to but not even including the index supplied as the second claim in the deletion loop. Using the unique constant tk.END is the second claim of the function. Delete (); you can eliminate all of the text in the entry. When calling.insert(), the first argument specifies where the text should be placed. Unless there is already text in the entry, a new line of text is always put at the widget's start, regardless of the value you supply as the first argument to the function. For example, if you had called. Insert () with one hundred as the first parameter rather than zero; the result would have been the same. The .insert() function will insert new text at the specified location and shift all current text to the right if the entry already has text. Because they only display on a single line, entry widgets are good for obtaining tiny amounts of information from a user, but they are less effective for gathering huge volumes of content. Text widgets are in handy in this situation!

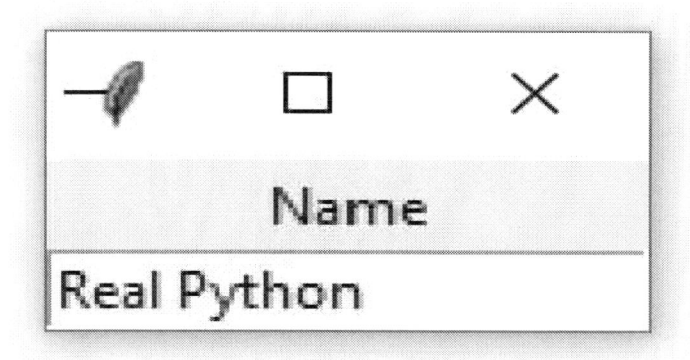

11.2: Making Your Applications Interactive

By now, you should have a solid understanding of how to construct a window using Tkinter, add basic widgets, and manage the entire layout of the application. That's fantastic, but programs shouldn't just look attractive; they should also perform some functions! Throughout this section, you'll learn how and where to bring your apps to life by having them do actions when certain events occur.

Using .bind()

When an event takes place on a widget, the .bind function can call an event handler (). Because the incident handler is called whenever the event happens, it is referred to as being bound to the event. You'll continue with the keypress sample from the previous section, but this time you'll use .bind() to bind handle keypress() to the keystroke event: handle keypress() will be called whenever a key is pressed.

.bind() always requires a minimum of two arguments:

1. An event is defined by a line of the type "event name>," where the event name might be any of the happenings available in Tkinter.

The function's name invoked whenever an event happens is designated as an event handler in step two. A binding is established between the event handler and the widgets on which the call to .bind() is made. It is possible to transmit events to event handler functions when they are called by calling the callback function. Although the event handler in the preceding example is connected to the window, you can bind a callback function to any widget in the application. For illustration, you can assign an event listener to a Button widget, which will cause the following action to be performed whenever the link is pressed.

Example Code

def handle_click(event):

   print("The button was clicked!")

button = tk.Button(text="Click me!")

button.bind("<Button-1>", handle_click)

Using command

Every Button widget includes a command attribute, which may be used to associate a function with it. When the button is pushed, the function is activated and conducted. Take a glance at an illustration. First, you'll need to construct a window containing a Label widget that contains a numeric value. The buttons will be placed on the left & right sides of the label. It will be necessary to use the left button to decrease its number in the label and the right button to increase the value.

11.3: Building a Temperature Converter

In this section, you'll create a temperature converting application that formats a temperature from degrees Fahrenheit and then press a button to convert the temperature to degrees Celsius, as seen in the screenshot. Throughout the tutorial, you'll be guided through code step-by-step. We've included the complete source code just at the end of this part for your reference. Before you begin coding, you'll need to create a design for your app. You'll need three components:

1. Temperature entry: Ent temperature is used to enter the Fahrenheit temperature.

2. A label is displayed using the LBL result widget, which stands for Celsius result.

3. Button: When a button is pressed, a widget named btn convert is activated, which reads the value first from the Entry widget, converts this from Celsius to Celsius, and updates the text of a Label widget to the result.

A single row and column can be used to organize the widgets in a grid format. It results in a marginally functional application, although it is not user-friendly. Everything must be labeled in some way. A label bearing the Fahrenheit sign (°F) will be placed directly to the side of the ent temperature widget so that the user is aware that the value of ent temperature is in degrees Fahrenheit. Change the label text to "DEGREE FAHRENHEIT," which displays the Fahrenheit symbol using Python's Unicode character support, available through the Unicode character support package.

The text "NRIGHTWARDS BLACK ARROW" can be used to decorate the btn convert button, which exhibits a black arrow to the right when the button is clicked. The Celsius symbol (°C) will always appear after the label text "N DEGREE CELSIUS" in the LBL result, indicating that the result is expressed in degrees Celsius. It is what the final panel will look like after it is finished. Now that you understand what widgets you'll need and how the window will look, you can start putting the code together! To begin, import Tkinter and build a new window as follows. An existing window's title can be changed using the window. Title () function, and the window. Resizable () function with both assertions set to False causes the window to have a fixed size. Upon completing the installation process, the window will display the words Temperature Conversion in its title bar. Afterward, construct the ent temperature widget and a label known as LBL temp, and then attach them to a Frame widget known as from entry.

The user will enter the Fahrenheit value into ent temperature, and the Fahrenheit symbol will be labeled in ent temperature by the function lbl temp. The ent temperature and LBL temperature containers are grouped into entry containers. All temperatures should be positioned right side of ent temperature as shown before. You can arrange them from entry using the .grid() geometry manager to arrange them in a single row and two columns. It will always attach to the rightmost border of its grid cell because you've set the persistent parameter for ent temperature to "e." In addition, you set the adhesive to "W" for all temperatures to ensure that it remains glued to the bottom left edge of its grid cell. It guarantees that LBL temp is always situated directly to the left of ent temperature. Create the buttons btn convert and LBL result to translate the temperature input into ent temperature to a different temperature and show the results. Both the btn convert and the LBL result buttons are assigned to the window, much like the firm entry. These three widgets are grouped to form the three cells of the main application's grid. Please use the .grid() function to lay them out right away. Finally, launch the application as follows. That is excellent! However, for the time being, the button accomplishes nothing. Add a Fahrenheit to Celsius feature to the top of your script file, directly just below the import line, and save the file (). When this task/function is called, it reads the data from the ent temperature variable, converts that from Fahrenheit into Celsius, and returns the result in the LBL result parameter.

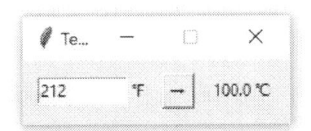

Chapter 12: Python and Web Development

Web design and development

The word "web development" refers to envisioning, designing, developing, implementing, and running web applications & application programming interfaces.

What is the significance of web development?

Since the first website went online in 1989, the Web has increased in terms of the number of sites, users, and implementation capabilities. Online development is a term that refers to all the actions that go into creating websites and web apps.

What part of web development does Python play?

Python is a programming computer language that may be present to create server-side web applications. Whereas a web framework isn't essential to creating web applications, it's uncommon for developers to not leverage existing open-source software to speed up the development process.

A web browser does not support Python. JavaScript is the programming computer language used by browsers like Chrome, Firefox, and Internet Explorer. Python to JavaScript compilers, such as pyjs, are available. On the other hand, most

Python website developers use a combination of Python & JavaScript to create their apps. Python is run on the server, while JavaScript was downloaded and run by the web browser on the client.

Resources for web development

To become an accomplished web developer, you'll need to understand HTTP requests and answers, the client (usually web browsers), & server (application server such as Nginx & Apache architectures, HTML, CSS, and JavaScript, among other things). The materials listed below provide a variety of viewpoints that, when combined, should help you obtain a better understanding of web development.

- How the Internet Works is also necessary for a rapid review of all the components that establish a network connection between two machines. The example demonstrates how to send an email, but the tale may also be used to learn about other connections, such as how to download a website.

- Knowing the core tools used to construct websites and online apps is essential to becoming a web developer. It's also crucial to remember that key ideas like HTTP, URLs, and HTML were there from the start and were later developed with additional standards. Starting with Tim Berners-original Lee's idea and release at CERN, this essay on the History of a Web briefly describes the beginnings of the Web.

- Web Architecture 101 is an excellent high-level overview of the technologies that power the contemporary Web, including DNS, load balancers, custom application servers (WSGI servers in Python), online databases, task queues, caching, and other key features topics.

- When does anything happen? It is an exceedingly complex solution to the question, "What transpires when you put google.com into the browser's address box & hit enter?" that seems simple but becomes more complicated as you delve deeper.

- How Browsers Work is a high-level overview of how browsers accept HTML, CSS, JavaScript, pictures, and other data as input and produce websites. Knowing these things is well worth your time as a web developer.

- The origins of the URL may be traced back to the ARPANET's expansion to hundreds of nodes, which finally led to the invention of the URL. It is an excellent read that offers historical background for why the Web is the way it is.

- The Instantly Loading Browser Hacker's Guide Everything is a fantastic technical presentation delivered by Addy that contains valuable developer information for both new and seasoned web developers.

- Develop a web program/application from the ground up, and its follow-up articles for request processing middleware delve further into the basics of web development. Even if you want to utilize an existing web framework like Django or Flask to create real-world apps, learning these core ideas is essential for a web developer.

12.1: Frameworks

Python web frameworks

What exactly are web frameworks, & why do they matter?

Consider a toolbox. A web framework is a set of standardized packages, pre-written, and modules that facilitate the building of online applications, making development quicker and simpler and your programs more stable and scalable. Put another way; frameworks contain built-in components that "set up" your project, so you don't have to operate as much hard Work.

Web frameworks written in Python are exclusively used in the backend for backend technologies like URL routing, Lookups and replies, database access, and web security. While using a web framework is not needed, it is highly recommended since it allows you to construct complicated apps in a fraction of the time.

What are some of the well-known(established) Python web frameworks?

The most python Programming web development frameworks are Django and Flask. Django is a Python website framework/agenda that "encourages quick development & clean, pragmatic design." It is an open-source, high-level framework. It's quick, safe, and expandable. Django has a large community & extensive documentation. Django is very adaptable, allowing you to deal with anything from MVPs to major corporations. Instagram, Pinterest, Dropbox, & Spotify are just a few of the top firms that utilize Django.

Flask is basic and lightweight, which means you may add extensions & libraries as you write rather than having them given by the framework. Flask's philosophy is to provide just the components that need to construct an app, giving you maximum freedom and control. Large organizations like Netflix, LinkedIn, & Uber utilize Flask, making it a popular and capable web framework.

Other noteworthy frameworks include:

- Pyramid
- Turbogears
- Web2Py

Which one should you go with?

As a result, you may wonder, "What framework should I choose?" The response is that it is dependent on the situation. Consider your degree of expertise as just a web developer. Consider starting with something more "barebones" if you have a lot of experience. However, a framework with greater help, such as Django, may be preferable if you're a new developer.

Also, consider if you'd rather have a "foundation" codebase to build on or the freedom to create the backbone of the codebase. Choose Django if you choose the first choice; Flask if you prefer a second one.

At the end of each day, they both can do the same tasks, and it's essential to get started writing than obsess about which framework is superior.

12.2: Django basics
Python Django Web Development

Learn the fundamentals of web programming by building blog apps with the Create, Read, Update(CRUD), & Delete feature using Django.

Django is a popular high-level website development framework that is free and open source. It gives developers several functionalities "out of the box," allowing for quick development. On the other hand, websites designed using it are safe, scalable, and easy to manage.

Setup is required.

1. Git Bash: It may be used on any operating system. It is via it that all Django and Unix operations are executed. Click Me to get the Git bash.

2. Text-Editor: You may use any text editor, such as

Sublime Text/Visual Studio Code. Sublime Text is used in the following project.

3. Python 3: Download Python to get the most recent version of Python.

Note: If you have a rudimentary understanding of Python and are familiar with loops, functions, classes, and other concepts, as well as some familiarity with shell or command line, you may easily follow through with this lesson.

Environment Virtual

Virtual Environments are Python-related projects' dependencies. It functions as an identity container or isolated environment that contains all the Python-related packages & needed versions for a certain project. Because newer versions of Django, Python, or packages, for example, will be released, you may work with earlier versions that are particular to your project using a Virtual Environment. In summary, you may start an individual assignment linked to Django version 2.0 on the same machine as another separate related project to Django version 3.0.

Note: There are other techniques to create a Virtual Atmosphere, but only one is shown here.

Conclusion

Congratulations on completing the lesson! You've mastered the fundamentals of Django Web Development & thus are familiar with the CRUD feature. Also, see the Django documentation for more information on a specific subject.

12.3: Future of web development

Is Python the Way to Build Web Apps in the Future?

Python is quickly gaining popularity as one of the most widely used programming languages. Python is currently the preferred web development language for businesses that need corporate applications, machine learning or artificial intelligence systems, or scalable online apps.

Python is the quickest programming language, according to Stack overflow's 2019 study. Python programs are powerful because the code is straightforward, precise, and easy to understand.

Many of today's online applications operate with data. Python programming helps businesses use this data and use Machine Learning to make more informed choices. Amazon, Hulu, Netflix, and a slew of other services are instances of data-driven development. A Python programming business may assist you in creating an app that is like one of these.

The following are a few advantages of Python regarding website development

The days of developers being headed by a single operating system are long gone. Python is just a cross-platform language, so you may employ Python developers & deploy them on any OS. It runs on Linux, Windows, and other operating systems. If the code is written on a Mac, this will execute well on a Windows machine.

Python web design services provide excellent libraries for extending the functionality of your website. Built-in functions, constant types, exceptions, GUI development tools, Scrappy, & a slew of other add-ons are all available. Plugins are used in

Python applications to save developers from writing code from scratch.

Python development programming is not exceedingly difficult, given the language's resilience. It is simple and easy to understand, popular among Python programmers. It takes advantage of white space indentation & does away with curly brackets. Python is a newcomer language, which is one of the reasons why everyone is using it to build websites.

The Python community for website designing is rapidly expanding. According to another Stack overflow study, it is one of the top five most popular programming languages among developers. The community helps resolve any problem. You will get frequent information about changes in the versions and solutions to various difficulties.

Python programming language's future

It may not be straightforward/easy to believe, but full-stack app development businesses will be on the same page. Data science is the most important factor in its rise.

Python comes with a toolset for creating AI and machine learning applications. Scientists can readily manipulate data sets using Python-based algorithms. There are many libraries for statistical computing, data analysis, & every other component of AI. Python libraries include PyBrain, Qury, PyAnn, MDP ToolKit, and GraphLab Create.

Ansible, Pyeapi, and Netmiko are a few packages that assist networking. Python web development isn't only for apps; it can also be used to easily set up routers. The Python programming language's foundation for website building is so robust that its other uses are still in early infancy.

Python allows programmers to create futuristic online applications and devices. The code is being used to develop complicated algorithms that turn plain Text into intelligent applications. You may start working on your Python project right now by hiring web application development services.

Companies such as Google, Netflix, Apple, and others choose to use the programming language. Invest in a robust Python application and become those firms.

Conclusion

Python is a fascinating and important computer programming language. It is popular among programmers because it is easy to learn and master. It features a straightforward user interface. You won't have to devote as much time to learning Python as you would to learning a different language. The Python engine can do various functions, and its frameworks come in a variety of forms, enabling users to be as creative as they want.

Even though major companies prefer quicker languages, Python has several features that make it a good choice for game development, App development, etc. Large companies widely use it for different purposes. Python is part of a larger set of data analytics abilities that can help you stand out as a more competitive candidate since information analysts need various talents. They must also gather, process, and analyze vast volumes of complex data, discover and forecast patterns, communicate their results, and cooperate with other teams within their businesses. After finishing these degrees, these graduates are qualified for positions such as data analysts, business analysts, and software engineers, to mention a few. More importantly, Python's enormous library of code libraries enables you to utilize code written by other programmers.

Python is a very capable programming language. Instead of being compiled before being run, the code is performed immediately. There are benefits & drawbacks to this, but one of the biggest benefits is that if the code has a mistake, the program will stop operating and show a single warning message. Concentrating on one problem, correcting it, and moving on is a huge assist in making debugging more manageable.

Python is a multi-platform general-purpose programming language with a user-friendly syntax. It is the most popular and fastest-growing programming language today due to its simplicity. It's used in several fields, including game creation, deep learning, and robotics. Easy development is critical for novice developers. Many individuals choose to learn Python, a coding language taught in intensive programs that usually concentrate on a certain set of coding languages and skillsets and allow you to learn at your speed. Python's active online community makes independent study options especially appealing - anybody interested in learning the language may benefit from the information and tools supplied by programmers who are willing to volunteer their time and skills online. Seeing results quickly, particularly when you're just starting, is all the encouragement you need to keep going!